$1⁰⁰

THE CABILDO

ON

JACKSON SQUARE

The Cabildo from the upper Pontalba Building.

THE CABILDO

ON JACKSON SQUARE

The Colonial Period

1723 - 1803

By Samuel Wilson, Jr.

The American Period

1803 to the present

By Leonard V. Huber

A FIREBIRD PRESS BOOK

PELICAN PUBLISHING COMPANY
Gretna 1998

Manufactured in the United States of America

Published by Pelican Publishing Company, Inc.

1000 Burmaster Street, Gretna, Louisiana 70053

Printed in U.S.A.

by Laborde Printing Company

New Orleans, La.

CONTENTS

Introduction

The Cabildo, one of the monumental buildings flanking the Basilica of St. Louis, is one of the most important historic buildings in the United States and undoubtedly the most important surviving monument of the period of Spanish domination in Louisiana. Its name is derived from the Spanish municipal governing body, or Cabildo, set up by Don Alexandro O'Reilly in 1769 to replace the Superior Council that had governed Louisiana during the French regime. Louisiana's second Spanish governor, O'Reilly, who firmly established Spanish rule in the former French colony, instituted a form of city government similar to that existing in major cities in Mexico and other Spanish colonies in Central and South America. The simple structure that O'Reilly had built here to house the Cabildo in 1769, was destroyed in the fire of 1788. Construction of its replacement, the present Cabildo, was begun in 1795. Only a few years after its completion in 1799 it was the setting for the ceremonies by which the Spanish colony was retroceded to France on November 30, 1803, and for similar ceremonies when it was transferred less than three weeks later to the United States by Napoleon's emissaries, on December 20, 1803. By this act of transfer the boundaries of the United States were extended to the Pacific Ocean. The Louisiana Purchase was the event that caused Robert R. Livingston to utter the words: "We have lived long, but this is the noblest work of our whole lives . . . The United States take rank this day among the first powers of the earth."

Wrought iron balcony rail from a side window of the Cabildo.

The First Corps de Garde (1723-1724)

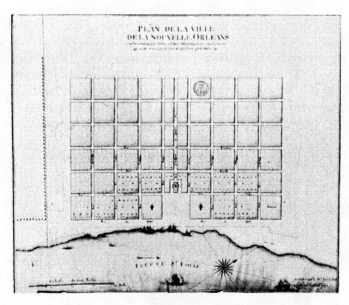

Plan of New Orleans by Le Blond de la Tour dated April 23, 1722.
Courtesy Bibliothèque Nationale, Paris.

The site upon which the Cabildo stands was set aside for government use when the plan of the new town of New Orleans was laid out in 1721 by the French military engineer, Adrien de Pauger, three years after the city was founded by Jean Baptiste Le Moyne de Bienville in 1718. The parish church was placed in the center of a symmetrical composition, the land on its other flank being set aside for religious use as a site for the presbytère or church rectory. These three contemplated units overlooking the public square or Place d'Armes, now Jackson Square, together with other proposed symmetrical structures to face the sides of the square, were to be the visual as well as administrative center of a new metropolis which Pauger unhesitatingly predicted "is going to become a great city."

Cutting and squaring of timbers for the first structures to occupy these three dominant sites at the back of the square was begun late in 1723. The first timbers to be delivered were those for the corps de garde or police station to be built at the corner of Chartres and St. Peter streets. The parish priests, however, complained so bitterly about their poor lodgings that Pauger transferred these timbers to the other side of the church site and by February 9, 1724 had erected "the framing of the house of the Capuchins . . . and it will be ready to occupy in the end of March . . ." The corps de garde was expected to be finished

1

shortly thereafter, a small structure of colombage construction, a pegged framework of heavy timbers covered on the outside with wide boards and roofed with wood shingles. Like the presbytère, it was about 40 feet in width and 20 in depth with a steeply pitched, hipped roof, typically French in character. Its location, size and shape are shown on many of the early maps of New Orleans, but the only view of it is included in the large perspective view of New Orleans in 1726 as drawn by Jean Pierre Lassus from the opposite side of the river. Here it is crudely represented as a small, one-story structure with a central door-

New Orleans as it was in 1726 from a drawing by Jean Pierre Lassus.
Courtesy Archives Nationales, Section Outremer, Paris.

way flanked by two windows, the presbytère being shown in identical form. In 1731 when the Company of the Indies gave up its control of Louisiana and retroceded the colony to the King, Louis XV, an inventory of buildings given up by the Company indicates that the presbytère had a filling of brick masonry added between its wall timbers, for greater solidity and insulation. It had double paneled entrance doors with a glazed transom and glazed windows with double batten shutters. Though not shown in the Lassus sketch, "a gallery . . . facing the square" had been added to both the presbytère and the corps de garde by Pauger in 1725. The corps de garde, completed in the latter part of that year by the architect Bernard Devergès, and the presbytère, were the first buildings facing the Place d'Armes to be finished, establishing the symmetry of the Square. The parish church, begun in 1724, was not completed until Christmas, 1727.

The Prisons (1729-1730)

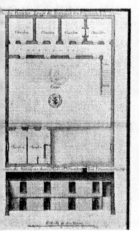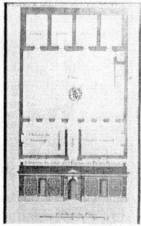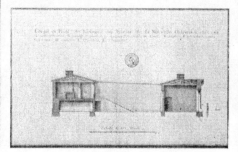

Plan, elevation and section of the prison of 1730 by Pierre Baron.

With the corps de garde or police station established, it was logical that a prison and courtroom should be constructed nearby. In August 1729, Etienne de Périer, who had succeeded Bienville as Commandant General, or governor of the colony, wrote that "We are beginning to work on the prison which will be entirely of brick". The new building, one of the first all-brick structures in New Orleans, was located facing the Square between the corps de garde and the church, on part of the site of the present Cabildo. It was undoubtedly designed by Pierre Baron, a naturalist sent by the Royal Academy of Sciences to do scientific research in Louisiana, who had, after his arrival, been made King's Engineer by Périer. An unsigned set of drawings, dated 14 January 1730, shows the completed prison building. It contained two separate units with the prison yard between them, enclosed at each end by a high brick wall. The front structure contained a central entrance passage from the street to the yard, with a high-ceilinged courtroom or *chambre criminelle* on the right and a two-story apartment for the *concierge* or gate keeper on the left.

In the rear of the yard was the cell block, a two-story structure containing four vaulted brick cells on the ground floor, with massive walls for maximum-security prisoners. Even these five-foot-thick walls did not prove to be impenetrable, for later records reveal that prisoners sometimes escaped by digging holes through the walls of the dungeon-like cells. The second story was reached

3

by a brick staircase from the yard and contained four smaller but more comfortable cells that opened from a corridor across the front of the building, from which they received borrowed light. Two of these cells were even provided with large open fireplaces; these were probably reserved for more distinguished prisoners or debtors. All windows of both front and back buildings opened into the prison yard, the only opening to the outside being the entrance gate. This arched gateway was of monumental proportions, flanked by pilasters and capped by a triangular pediment. The flanking blank walls were relieved by large niches or false windows, decorative brick panels and brick quoins. Most of this brick work of the façade was left exposed but the remainder of the building was plastered to protect the soft local brick from the effects of the weather.

Although there are records of criminal trials in New Orleans as early as 1720, references to the imprisonment of criminals are comparatively rare. The Attorney General or prosecuting attorney, François Fleuriau, conveniently lived on a large property just back of the corps de garde and the prison, the lot bounded on its other sides by St. Peter, Royal and Orleans streets. In 1728 he brought to trial, one Jean Melun, accused of stabbing a man who caught him in the act of robbing a house. Fleuriau asked for conviction and punishment by flogging by the public executioner at the street crossings and banishment from the colony forever. At the end of the trial, the accused's wife presented a touching appeal for clemency on the grounds of her husband's drunkenness and insanity. This trial and the confinement of the accused probably took place in the corps de garde, for the prison and criminal courtroom had not as yet been built.

In a murder trial in 1766 the record indicates that the accused was brought to New Orleans from Natchitoches where the crime occurred and confined to the prison with irons on his hands and feet. The accused, Michel Degout, a master sculptor, had used one of his tools in killing a man named Cratte in a fight. Convicted of the crime, he was sentenced to be led through the streets in a cart to be then brought to a scaffold on the public square, broken on a wheel and left to die, his body then to be exposed on the public road. Mercifully the court ordered that the condemned "be strangled under the scaffold before receiving a blow". This sentence was carried out on February 1, 1766. It was in the criminal courtroom *(chambre criminelle)*, on the site of the present Cabildo that murder trials like this were held, and from the prison back of it that the condemned were led to execution on the public square.

4

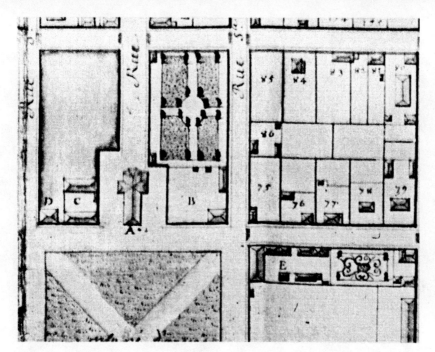

Detail of Gonichon's plan of 1731 showing the original corps de garde built in 1723 (D) and the prison and criminal courtroom (C).

Courtesy Archives Nationales, Section Outremer, Paris.

The New Corps de Garde (1751)

After nearly thirty years of use, the little police station or corps de garde of brick between posts construction, at the corner of Chartres and St. Peter streets, was replaced with a more substantial building. As had happened with most of the other early French buildings in New Orleans, its timbers had eventually rotted away. The intendant Michel in May, 1751 informed the French court that "It is indispensable that we work on rebuilding the corps de garde on the public square of this town, which is too small and which is falling down. Work is to be done there without delay."

The first work was the construction of a temporary structure, "the building where the guard on the Place d'Armes is housed while waiting until the new corps de garde might be built." Financial records for the year 1752 list payments for this work which probably included demolition of the old corps de garde.

The new building was designed by Ignace Broutin and by Bernard Devergès, who succeeded him as Engineer-in-Chief of Louisiana after Broutin's death in August 1751. The contractor

The corps de garde of 1751. Parts of its walls are incorporated in the present Cabildo.
Restorative Drawing by Henry W. Krotzer, Jr.

for the new corps de garde as well as for the temporary one was
Claude Joseph Villars Dubreuil, who was at this time just completing the new convent for the Ursuline nuns down Chartres
Street. The plans and specifications were dated August 21, 1750
and the construction contract was signed on September 17 following . The new corps de garde, like the convent, was entirely
of brick masonry, about forty-two and a half feet wide, facing
the public square and about fifty-eight feet in depth along St.
Peter Street. The gable end wall of the prison building and the
high wall of the prison yard, both of which were rebuilt, formed
the side wall of the new structure. Across the front was a gallery
about fourteen feet deep with four massive square columns with
pedestals, moulded bases and capitals. The gallery floor was
paved with bricks laid on edge, two steps above the sidewalk
level. The sidewalks or banquettes in front and on the St. Peter
Street side were paved with bricks laid flatwise, with borders
and gutters. Two pairs of heavy wood batten doors with transom
bars and glazed fan transoms above, led from the gallery into
the building which was divided ·by a heavy brick wall into two
long rooms. This division wall was pierced by five arches, opposite each of which, in the St. Peter Street wall, was a window
protected with a wrought iron grille of heavy square bars. These

6

windows, which had no glazed sash, were closed only by heavy wood batten shutters.

At the far end of each of the two divisions of the corps de garde, opposite the entrance doors, was a large open fireplace. A door to the left of the fireplace on the St. Peter Street side, led to a smaller room in back that served as quarters for the jailor. Another door led into the old prison building where in 1753 Dubreuil had fitted up a room for the officer of the guard, opening up the false windows of the original design to provide light and a view of the Square. A wooden staircase in the rear of the corps de garde gave access to the large attic. Under the stair were two cells, probably for the temporary detention of prisoners brought in off the street by the guard. The floor, like the floor of the gallery, was of brick on edge, laid in a running bond with borders and cross strips, one brick wide, dividing the large areas into smaller rectangular spaces. The ceiling was of the exposed wooden beams and wide, tongue-and-groove, beaded boards that formed the attic floor. The attic was framed with heavy timber trusses, the rafters sheathed on the inside with wide beaded boards, and must have closely resembled the attic of the Ursuline convent.

The corps de garde was sparsely furnished and contained four wooden gun-racks. Two similar racks were provided outside under the portico and several were built in the attic which served as an arsenal. A storeroom was built in the attic "to serve for depositing boxes of cartridges and other munitions." Five dormer windows with glazed sash in the attic, three probably centered above three of the windows of the St. Peter Street façade, and two in the hipped end facing the Place d'Armes, admitted ample light to this large attic space. Outside, the roof was covered with small flat tiles like those still to be seen on a few old roofs in the Vieux Carré, such as the Girod house at Chartres and St. Louis streets. The rear wall towards Royal Street was in the form of a gable with the two fireplace chimneys rising above it. The jailer's quarters formed a wing extending back along St. Peter Street about twenty feet. It was twenty-two feet wide with a fireplace backed against one of the fireplaces of the corps de garde. The jailer's room had three shuttered windows like those of the main building but without the iron grilles. Two of these windows opened onto St. Peter Street and one onto the prison yard. These windows were provided with double casement sashes, covered with cloth instead of glass, like the earliest New Orleans buildings. The room also had three doors, one opening into the corps de garde, one to the prison yard and one to the street.

Besides the arms racks, the corps de garde was also furnished with built-in "camp beds." These were wide, slightly sloping platforms elevated some two to three feet above the floor. The frames were of heavy structural timbers and the platforms were of tongue and groove beaded boards of the same type used for the attic floor. Beds of this type are shown on several Devergès drawings, including the proposed corps de garde at the Balise drawn by him in 1734 and the corps de garde at Fort Tombigbee in 1761. The guardsmen lay on blankets on these hard boards for the little sleep they were allowed when on duty. A long table and benches of the type shown on the Tombigbee drawings probably completed the furnishings of the New Orleans corps de garde.

Following France's cession of her Louisiana colony to Spain, a general inventory of all her properties, buildings, etc. being transferred by the French King to his Spanish cousin was made in 1766-67 by representatives of both countries. Included were "The buildings of the corps de garde of the Place d'Armes and of the prisons, civil as well as military." This inventory describes in minute detail every element of the corps de garde. Similarly inventoried were "The building of the military prisons, the military criminal chamber, the civil criminal chamber, the privies for the use of the prisons, civil as well as military and for the corps de garde . . . and all the enclosure or encircling walls of these buildings." Finally the inventory describes "The building opposite the Place d'Armes, adjoining the corps de garde, serving as a chamber for the officer of the guard and lodging for the jailer of the civil prison."

The land on which the Cabildo stands today was listed separately in the first part of the inventory, dated April 2, 1766, as

The land of the new corps de garde of the Place d'Armes, containing twenty toises [120 feet] front to the river, by 30 [180 feet] of depth, on which stand the said corps de garde, the chamber of the officer of the guard, the civil and military prisons, the criminal chambers of the two said prisons, the lodgings for the jailers, their privies and those for the use of the corps de garde.

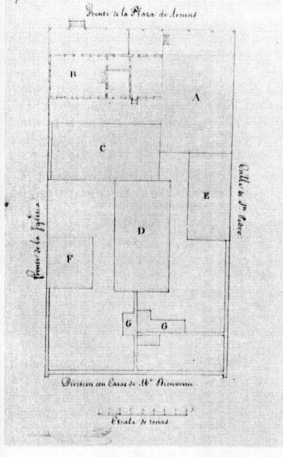

Plan of the corps de garde (A), prisons (C), and first Cabildo (B), being constructed in 1769.

Courtesy Rosemonde E. and Emile Kuntz Collection. Manuscripts Section, Tulane University Library.

New Prisons and Council Chamber (1753)

At the time the corps de garde was built, the same contractor, Joseph Dubreuil also did extensive remodeling to the old prison that had been built by Baron in 1730. The old courtroom, or *chambre criminelle,* was converted into an apartment for the jailer of the civil prison with an upper story or mezzanine. His former quarters in the same front building, which also had a mezzanine floor, were converted into quarters for the officer of the guard, adjoining the corps de garde, a doorway between the two buildings being provided. The room behind the corps de garde, facing on St. Peter Street, became the quarters for the jailer of the military prison and was later enlarged by the addition of another room with its fireplace, the same size of the original room, behind it and separated from it by a passageway leading from St. Peter Street into the courtyard of the military prison.

A *toisé* or survey and evaluation of the work on the old prison made by the engineer Devergès, dated December 31, 1753 also describes the building of the wall and vault that forms a corridor in front of the cells on the ground floor of the rear building, "for masking the doors of the cells in the yard". Dubreuil was also paid "to re-do its paving anew, as well as the framing timbers of the floors and roofs that have rotted at these two buildings." Other work done included "rebuilding an opening that has been made in an outside wall in the small cell under the staircase by a prisoner who escaped."

Some additional work was also done at this time for furniture "at the chamber of the officer of the guard of the new corps de garde of the Place d'Armes," including "the furnishing of a table three feet long by two feet two inches wide, with its drawer fitted with its lock" and "two iron hoops six feet in length, with staples for the mosquito bar, together with the labor for having taken down the camp bed in the old corps de garde and having transported it and set it up again in the new chamber . . ."

In the budget of expenses for 1754, submitted by the *Ordonnateur* D'Auberville on November 22, 1753 was an item of 5,000 *livres,*

> for final payment for a large corps de garde, a new military prison, criminal chambers, cells, privies, enclosure and separation walls, the whole built of brick.

Included in the 1764 budget was an amount "for an extension to be made to the criminal chamber in order to make a depository for the papers of the recorder".

After Don Alexandro O'Reilly had become Governor in 1769 and firmly established Spanish rule in Louisiana, he ordered a new inventory and re-appraisal made "of all the buildings that belonged to His Most Christian Majesty in the Plaza of New Orleans and its vicinity." Accompanying this inventory, completed in 1772, was a series of drawings showing each of the royal properties and the location of the buildings that then existed upon them. On one of these drawings (page 9), "the new town hall that is being constructed," to house the new Spanish Cabildo, is shown adjacent to the corps de garde where, until then, stood the front part of the 1730 prison building housing the officer of the guard and the jailer of the civil prison. Back of it, the military prison is shown attached to the rear of the old rear prison building. It was a two-story building of brick construction, roofed with flat tiles. The military criminal chamber, or courtroom was probably located in this same building while the civil courtroom was in another structure adjacent to Orleans Street facing the church, marked *Old Council Chamber*. This building probably

Alexandro O'Reilly, an Irishman in the service of Spain, came to New Orleans on August 18, 1769, with 2,600 Spanish troops to begin the Spanish regime.

also housed the Superior Council which until then met in a small council chamber behind *La Direction,* the old administration building built in 1722 near the corner of what is now Toulouse and Decatur.

On January 17, 1732, *Ordannateur* Salmon had proposed such a building and pointed out the advantages to be gained "when I shall have had a Council Chamber constructed adjoining the prisons, the building today being of only planks and not being able to endure more than two or three years." The French Superior Council was in fact a court rather than a governing body; the king on September 2, 1732, pointing out that "this council must not take part directly or indirectly with what concerns the government and the general administration of the colony, and that he has submitted to it a part of his authority only for the purpose of rendering justice to his subjects in matters of dispute."

In the Superior Council Chamber occurred the stirring events of 1768 that led to the revolt against Spain, and it may have been, at least for a while, in the cells of either the civil or military prisons that the leaders of the rebellion were confined during their trial for treason. Don Alexandro O'Reilly had taken formal possession of the colony for Spain on August 18, 1769 with pomp and ceremony and display of military might in the public square, which henceforth became known as the *Plaza de Armas.*

11

Immediately after the ceremonies in the public square, Spanish troops occupied the corps de garde and the city fortifications. On August 21, O'Reilly had the leaders of the revolt arrested and at first imprisoned on ships of his fleet and in "a well-guarded house". The trial itself possibly took place in one of the *chambres criminelles* or courtrooms within the prison compound. The Louisiana historian, Charles Gayarré, whose great-grandfather Don Estevan de Gayarré, had arrived in New Orleans in 1766 as Spanish Royal Auditor and Comptroller, describes the trial, in which "the judges descended into the cells of the accused and forced them to answer minutely all the questions they deemed proper to propound . . ." On October 24, 1769, the court found the prisoners guilty. Five men were sentenced to death, one had died while imprisoned, presumably killed by his guards, one sentenced to life in prison, two to ten years and three to six years. The five leaders were condemned "to the ordinary pain of the gallows . . . to be led to the place of execution, mounted on asses, and each one with a rope around his neck, then and there to be hanged until death ensue." No hangman could be found to execute the sentence so the penalty was changed to death by a firing squad. This was carried out on October 25. The next day all copies found of the printed "Memorial . . . of the Inhabitants of Louisiana", the revolutionary manifesto, were burned on the public square by the Spanish Clerk of Court. This notable event in Louisiana history, this first American revolution, is commemorated by a bronze plaque on the front of the Cabildo.

Spanish Coat of Arms, 1773.

The First Cabildo Building (1769)

The first Cabildo. Constructed in 1769, this building served until 1788 when it was destroyed in the great fire — Restorative sketch by Henry W. Krotzer, Jr., from the description in the specifications by Don Luis Andry.

One of O'Reilly's first official acts as governor was the abolishing of the old French Superior Council and the establishment of a Spanish Cabildo for the government of the city. To house this new governing body he ordered the construction of a new town hall, signing a contract for it on December 11, 1769 with a builder, François Hery, called Duplanty. According to the specifications accompanying this contract, the new building was to be "sixty-two feet long and twenty-four feet wide . . . to serve as Town Hall. This building is to be constructed on the site of the one that serves today as corps de garde to the officer of the guard at the Place d'Armes and as lodging to the jailer of the Civil Prisons. This old building will be first demolished to ground level . . ."

The new Town Hall was built on the foundations of the old structure, but was only of brick between posts or *colombage* construction, with a gallery across the front, an extension of the gallery of the corps de garde but with simple chamfered wood columns, bracketed at the top, instead of the great square masonry pillars of the older building. The plan was extremely simple. At the end of the building, nearer the church, was an Audience Hall, thirty feet in length by about twenty-three in width. At the opposite end was "an antechamber or waiting room for citizens requiring justice," eighteen feet in length by the same width as the Audience Hall. Between these two principal rooms was a seven-foot-wide connecting corridor, behind which a room about twelve by fifteen feet served as Archives. A large open fireplace furnished heat to the Audience Hall.

13

Between the columns of the gallery was a wood railing "fitted along the façade towards the Square as well as along that towards the church, with flat balusters made of planks cut out in profile, in good taste". A board partition across the gallery separated the public entrance from that of the judges. The roof was hipped at the end towards the church while the opposite end abutted the corps de garde. The roof, covered with wood shingles, was framed directly on the gallery columns and on the rear wall with equal slopes front and back. Every detail of the construction of this important colonial structure is minutely described in the specifications prepared by the Royal Surveyor, Don Luis Andry on December 9, 1769. Andry's plans, mentioned therein, have not been found.

The builder of this first Cabildo building, referred to in Spanish records as Don Francisco Hery, was a Frenchman who had been in the colony for many years. He had married Madeleine Brazillier in 1741 and their plantation on Bayou St. John, later acquired by Louis Allard, is now part of New Orleans's City Park. The price agreed upon for the new building was eighteen hundred piastres for which Hery accepted the concession of two

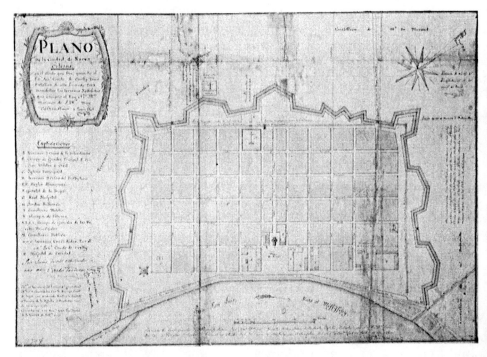

Plan by Carlos Trudeau made in 1801 to show the city as it existed when O'Reilly took possession of it in 1769.

Courtesy Louisiana State Museum.

14

squares of ground extending from Decatur to Royal between Iberville and Bienville, the site of the old Government House formerly occupied by Governor Vaudreuil, valued at twenty-five hundred piastres. Hery agreed to pay the difference of seven hundred piastres over a four-year period. Soon after completing his contract, Hery died and was given the unusual distinction of being buried inside the adjacent parish church of St. Louis.

The new Cabildo building, often referred to as the *Casa Capitular* or Council House, was accepted on August 17, 1770. The Illustrious Cabildo until then had held its sessions in the house of its President, Governor-General O'Reilly, where it had held its first meeting on December 1, 1769. At this first session six members were sworn into office, all former French officials or prominent citizens. Each swore to faithfully carry out the duties of his new office: "the right hand placed over the cross and on the Bible, he said that he swore and offered to God and the King, to defend the mystery of the Immaculate Conception of the Virgin Mary, to obey the orders and royal edicts of the King . . ." At this same session Don Luis de Unzaga y Amezaga, Colonel of the Royal Armies and Governor-Elect, was also sworn in to act in O'Reilly's place when necessary. The weekly sessions continued to be held at the Governor's house until the new building was made ready to be occupied. The last such meeting was held on August 31, 1770 and the following week, on September 7, the Cabildo met for the first time in its new *Casa de Ayuntamiento* or City Hall.

The records of the Cabildo for its meeting of September 28, 1770 in the *Casa Capitular* state that:

> It was brought to the attention of this Council the necessity of obtaining furniture and fixtures for the use of the Council Chamber and for the files in the Archives, to keep the books, papers, Cabildo documents, etc., and to this effect they agreed to have a large and strong book case made, to be closed with a lock, and some shelves for the papers and also a desk for the use of the Secretary; also to obtain some curtains and some other fixtures for the Cabildo's room in accordance with the dignity and convenience of the chamber . . . After this it was agreed that the Finance Commissioner pay for the book cases, curtains, tables and rugs, also the sixteen chairs that are needed for the use of the Council Chamber.

On November 9, 1770, a Mr. Duforest was paid nearly 730 livres for his work in furnishing and beautifying the Council Chamber; Mr. Bijou, a carpenter was paid 250 livres for building "a cabinet to store books, documents, etc., two tables, one large for the Council and another smaller one for the use of the Secretary." Mr. Desjean, a local blacksmith, was paid 40 livres for the iron rods on which to hang the curtains. A week later the Council also agreed to pay for a set of firedogs, a shovel and a pair of tongs for the fireplace. It also approved an expenditure for proper uniforms for the Cabildo's porters, for it was agreed that "these expenses were indispensable and that it was necessary to dress them as is customary in all cities of the Kingdom." The porters were also furnished with silver badges made in Havana at a cost of 447 pesos.

A year after it was ordered, the fireplace equipment had not yet been delivered and on November 9, 1771 the Cabildo stated that because of "the severity of the cold . . . [it was] dangerous to remain without fire in the Council Room of the City Hall", and demanded immediate procurement of the necessary equipment and firewood. On November 29 that year, "the blacksmith Desjean was paid twelve pesos for the iron dogs, shovel and tongs that he made for the Council Chamber in the City Hall."

Public festivals were celebrated with colorful ceremonies, the illumination of the City Hall being one of the features. On January 10, 1772 an account in the amount of sixty-three pesos, 6 reales, was "presented by Don Juan Durel for the cost of lighting the City Hall for the three nights that it was illuminated . . . during the celebration of the birth of His Highness, the Prince." A lesser amount was spent that summer in celebrating the Feast of St. John. The King's birthday was another occasion for decorating the building, various ornaments. and hangings and a profusion of gold braid being employed in this colorful celebration. In October, 1775 the building was again illuminated to celebrate the birth of the Infanta, daughter of the Prince of Asturias.

On February 14, 1774, the members of the Cabildo agreed "for the dignity of this Illustrious body, to order a velvet portière, trimmed with gold lace, to be made, together with the portrait of His Majesty (Whom God Preserve) and another one of the Prince of Asturias." Only a week before, they had approved a bill for whitewashing the exterior of the Casa Capitular. The next year, being pleased with the King's portrait that now hung in the Council Chamber, they decided that "other pictures will be placed in other chambers."

These colonial officials were proud of their position and carried out their functions with all the pomp and ceremony possible. One of the more curious ceremonies was enacted whenever a communication was received, signed by the King of Spain. Such a ceremony took place on March 11, 1774 when "a commission of confirmation, issued by His Majesty, was presented in favor of Don Andrés Almonester Estrada y Roxas, as Notary Public

Don Bernardo de Gálvez (1756-1786), fourth Spanish governor of Louisiana.

of War and Royal Treasury, which the Royal Ensign [one of the officers of the Cabildo] took in his hands,‹ kissed, made obeisance and placed it upon his head, as ordered by the King.'' The document was then read by the Secretary, J. B. Garic, and re-orded in the books of the Cabildo.

In 1777 Governor Unzaga was promoted to become Governor of Caracas and was succeeded by Don Bernardo de Gálvez. It was Gálvez who led his troops against the British and captured from them Fort Manchac, Baton Rouge, Natchez, Mobile and Pensacola in victories that are considered part of the American Revolution. Official news of these victories was received in the Council Chamber, the Cabildo ordering a *Te Deum* in thanksgiving to be sung in the parish church. At the conclusion of these campaigns, on April 14, 1782 there was general rejoicing, with a Mass of thanksgiving, *Te Deum* and procession and illumination of the public buildings.

Gálvez, in recognition of his accomplishments, was made Captain General of Louisiana and West Florida, and eventually Cuba. Spending most of his time in Cuba and elsewhere in the province, he designated Don Esteban Miró to take over the duties of Acting Military and Civil Governor during his own prolonged absence from New Orleans. On March 1, 1782 the Cabildo, in session in the Council Chamber, received Gálvez's instructions from Havana and with some reluctance, invited Miró to enter and take the oath of office. In 1785 Gálvez was made Viceroy of Mexico and Miró became Governor of Louisiana. On April 22, 1785, Don Andrés Almonester y Roxas appeared before the members of the Cabildo and announced his gift to the city of a hospital for lepers, one of his many philanthropic endeavors.

*Charles III, King of Spain
(1716-1788)
Louis XV, King of France ceded
Louisiana to him in 1762 and
Charles's rule of the colony ended
in the same year that the first great
fire destroyed a large part of New
Orleans.*

*From a painting by
Antoine Raphael Mengs
in the Prado Museum,
Madrid.*

The Fires of 1788 and 1794

By the beginning of the year 1787, the little building built by
O'Reilly in 1769 to house the Cabildo had begun to show the signs
of deterioration so common to buildings of brick-between-posts
construction. On February 23, 1787 the members of the Cabildo
discussed "The erection of a new building for the Cabildo and
decided to submit two plans for the building to be constructed;
one, in case it is decided to build it over the present chamber
of the Cabildo and corps de garde, and the other in the front
of the plaza facing the river if it was found more convenient,
in order that the cost of either building can be calculated and
the proper representation made to His Majesty, together with
the reasons which demand a new *Casa de Ayuntamiento* (City
Hall), in order to obtain his Royal permission."

It is interesting to note that the possibility of building a new
building over the old structure on the site was being considered
at this time, and that the site between the public square and the
river, opposite the church, was even proposed. Some preliminary
plans may have been drawn up but nothing had been decided
when on March 21, 1788 the building and a large part of the town

were destroyed in the terrible conflagration that occurred on the afternoon of Good Friday.

The fire began less than a block away from the Cabildo in the house of Don Joseph Vincent Nùñez, the Royal Treasurer, located up Chartres Street (now 619) opposite the garden of the Government House. According to the records of the Cabildo,

the fire started with such fury due to a strong south wind, it was impossible to control it until four hours later, during which time four-fifths of the populated section of the city was reduced to ashes, including the parish church and rectory, the Cabildo and the jail.

A letter from New Orleans dated March 26, 1788, published in the *London Chronicle* in August of that year, states that

the fire broke out at a large house (the treasurer's) not far from the church, which burned with irresistible fury, and communicating to the adjacent buildings, soon reached the guard house [corps de garde], from thence to the Church . . .

According to Governor Miró's report,

the parochial church and the Presbytère were among those struck by this misfortune, and the majority of their books have been destroyed by the fire. The *Casa Capitular* [Cabildo], the *Vivac* [watch house or corps de garde] and the *Sala de Armas* [the armory] with all the arms that were kept there, have all suffered the same fate, with the exception of seven hundred and fifty muskets. The public jail has also been burned and there was barely time to save the lives of the unfortunates locked therein; this was accomplished at the risk of our lives.

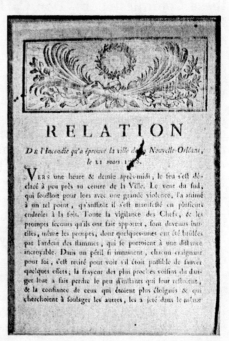

First printed ammount of the Great Fire of March 21, 1788, printed at Cap-Français, St. Domingue.

> *Broadside from the collection and by courtesy of Felix H. Kuntz.*

Thus on this dreadful afternoon O'Reilly's Cabildo building of 1769 was completely destroyed and the corps de garde with its armory and the civil and military prisons were destroyed with the exception of some of their massive brick walls which evidently remained standing. The records of the Cabildo were saved and the Cabildo established its meeting place temporarily in the Government House at Toulouse and Decatur, where its first session after the fire was held on March 26, 1788. At this time it was resolved that

> the jail being a place that contributes to the security of the public, the repairs of the same be entrusted without delay to the Chief Constable making use of city funds . . . and . . . to appoint two Commissioners to inspect the repairs to be made . . .

Despite the apparent urgency of these repairs little had been accomplished by August 22 that year when the subject was again brought up by the members of the Cabildo:

> The need of repairing the roof and the interior of the jail of this city was discussed not only for the public security and comfort of the prisoners, but also for the preservation of the walls that have been left standing since the fire . . . which would deteriorate to their foundations from water passing through them . . .

Again two members were appointed to take charge of making estimates of the repairs to be made. Finally on January 30, 1789 these Commissioners, Don Carlos de Reggio and Don Francisco Pascalis de la Barre presented to the Cabildo

> a plan of the necessary repairs for the accommodation of the prisoners and the preservation of the walls that were left standing after the fire . . .

It was then agreed to advertise for bids for this work. In the meantime a contract for repairs to the jailer's quarters had been let to Robert Jones, master carpenter, who on November 14, 1788 requested payment of 2450 pesos, having "complied well and faithfully with the conditions of the contract." It was not until March 13, 1789 that the contract for the repairs to the royal jail was awarded to Don Augustin de Macarty. Eight months later on November 27, Macarty reported to the Cabildo that he

> has finished rebuilding the royal jail which work was awarded him for 3250 pesos — plus the value of 279 pounds of iron that he furnished for the bars . . .

The work was duly inspected and payment authorized a week later. By May 14, 1790, Macarty had not yet been paid and again appealed to the Cabildo to honor its obligation, which finally it did.

After the destruction of the parish church in the fire of 1788, services were temporarily held in the chapel of the Charity Hospital. Located at the end of Toulouse Street, just inside the fortifications (now Rampart Street), this chapel proved to be too small and too far from the center of town. Governor Miró, at the request of the Bishop, Cirillo de Barcelona, reported in a letter of August 10, 1790 that he had given him "the use of the building that served as the guardhouse [corps de garde] of this post, and which had been adorned with great propriety . . ." The old corps de garde must by this time have been restored with a new roof and other fire damage repaired. It served then as the parish church of New Orleans almost until the new cathedral, built on the site of the old church, was completed and dedicated on Christmas Eve, 1794. Just two weeks before this, on December 8, the city was struck by another disastrous fire.

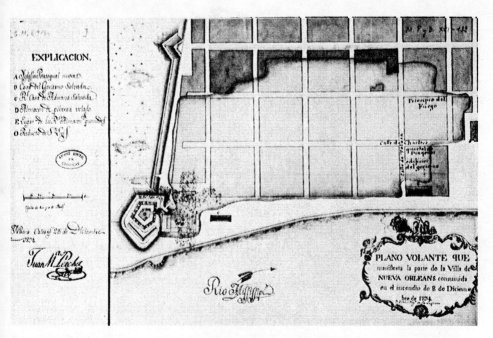

Plan showing that part of the city of New Orleans destroyed by the fire of December 8, 1794, as drawn by Juan M. Perchet, December 25, 1794, from Archivo General de Simancas, Spain.

Starting on Royal Street, the fire spread rapidly down until it reached practically to the wall of the new cathedral, again destroying the corps de garde and the royal jail as well as the fire engine house that the Cabildo had on March 1, 1793,

agreed to have Don Espíritu Liotau construct out of lumber, on the lot where the Cabildo building was burned, building it with as many doors as there are fire engines.

When the engine house was completed on November 1793 by Liotau and Favre & Co., they protested the estimate of it made by Don Gilberto Guillemard and Don Carlos Laveau Trudeau for the city. They named as their appraisers the master carpenters Robert Jones and Joseph Fernandez; both sides agreed on Don Lorenzo Wiltz as arbitrator. On December 20, 1793 his appraisal at 466 pesos was approved. In a little less than a year the engine house, that had so briefly stood on the site of the old Cabildo, was destroyed by the fire that destroyed the upper part of the city, from Orleans Street as far up as the fortifications (now Canal Street) and as far back as Bourbon Street, sparing only the Government House at Toulouse and Decatur and the house of Don Juan Francisco Merieult in that area, now 529 Royal.

François Louis Hector, Baron de Carondelet, a French nobleman in the Spanish service, governed Louisiana from 1792 to 1797.

By this time François Louis Hector, Baron de Carondelet, had become governor, succeeding Miró in December 1791. In his report on the fire, he stated that, although the number of buildings destroyed was not as great as in the fire in 1788, the monetary loss was infinitely greater because of the destruction of so many stores and commercial structures, as well as the royal powder magazine and parts of the new fortifications he had built soon after his arrival. He reported also the destruction of

> the jail, the building that served as a provisional church, the house in which the Capuchin Friars lived, the stables, the barracks of the dragoons and the servants' quarters of the Government House and many other buildings, the redoubt of *Fort San Luis* having suffered considerably.

In another report dated December 28, 1794, Carondelet gave his vivid eye-witness account. Hearing the cries of fire from some of the servants, he wrote,

> I ran to the principal guard house where the six pumps of the city were kept, and found that the Sergeant-Major of the town, Don Gilberto Guillemard, was leaving [with the pumps] for the place of the fire.

He then described the futile efforts to control the blaze.

> Prisoners were employed from the very beginning of the fire, in working the pumps and providing them with water, which necessarily had to be taken from a distance, for most of the private wells were empty and the Mississippi was low . . . We owe to the zeal and alertness of Don Nicolas Verbois, a lieutenant of the Army and commandant of the post of Iberville, the saving of the main building of the Government House, of which the stable and other buildings were completely burned.

All of the work that had been done on the corps de garde, the prisons, and the jailer's quarters, the fire engine house and other buildings that stood on the Cabildo site was again reduced to ashes. The church that had been set up temporarily in the old corps de garde was relocated after the fire in the chapel of the Ursulines until the new cathedral was ready to be dedicated. Again the first priority in rebuilding was given to the restoration of the prisons and the jailer's quarters. Within a week Guillemard had drawn up plans, specifications and estimates for rebuilding the roof for the jailer's quarters behind the corps de garde and for other necessary repairs to the prison. At the meeting of the Cabildo on December 12, 1794 "the urgent necessity of repairing the royal jail of this city was discussed . . . and they agreed that a plan be submitted by the two engineers of this city, together with an estimate of the cost." Guillemard, complying with this resolution, immediately prepared the plan and on December 16, 1794 "the plan for the repairs of the public jail was presented . . . approved . . . and placed at the head of the proceedings." The contract was awarded for 1130 pesos to Barthélemy Lafon who began work at once. On January 16, 1795 he requested a payment of 550 pesos on account "for repairing the royal jail, the greatest part of which work has been done, and if it was not for many days of bad weather and holidays, would be totally completed." The work was finished and final payment authorized on March 13, 1795, Lafon declaring that "some days ago a certain number of prisoners have been transferred to the said jail."

Not all of the prison buildings were included in Lafon's contract for repairs, so on May 9, 1795 the Cabildo again discussed "the indispensable necessity of repairing the roof of the upper rooms of the royal jail in order to protect the arches of the cells and restore the four upper rooms so the prisoners can be separated and also have an upper room for women, to which they unanimously agreed . . . roofing same with tiles. For this purpose the Sergeant Major of this plaza, Don Gilberto Guillemard, must make a plan and post a notice, fixing the 18th of the present month as a day on which the contract will be adjudicated." On this contract the lowest bidder was Robert Jones whose low bid of 1230 pesos was accepted. The repairs here were evidently for the rear building, the former military prison that had been built at about the time the corps de garde was constructed in the 1750's. After a long delay it was found that suitable tiles for the roof repairs could not be obtained locally and on August 14, 1795 the Cabildo confirmed a resolution "in regard to the covering of the royal jail with shingles (considering the urgent necessity of providing shelter from the rain for the prisoners) until the necessary tiles arrive from Havana, as those offered by Andrés Almonester y Roxas are of bad quality . . ." The shingle roof was immediately finished and Jones paid an adjusted sum for the less expensive wood shingles.

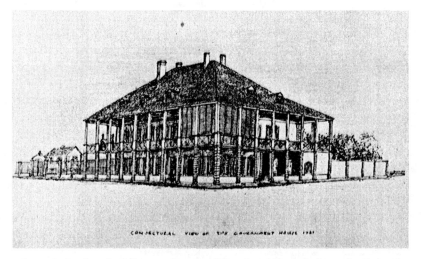

CONJECTURAL VIEW OF THE GOVERNMENT HOUSE 1761

One of the last buildings constructed by the French before the Spanish regime was the Government House which occupied a site on Decatur and Toulouse streets. Built in 1761, this building escaped the great fires of 1788 and 1794 and was used for a time by the Illustrious Cabildo as a meeting place. The structure served well into the American regime as the Louisiana capitol until it burned in 1828.

The Government House, (ca. 1800) A conjectural sketch made from contemporary drawings by Henry W. Krotzer, Jr.

After the fire of 1788, the Illustrious Cabildo at first held its sessions in the Government House which had escaped the fire, and where it had met from the time it was organized in 1769 until its original and now destroyed building was completed. On July 4, 1788 the subject of rebuilding was first seriously discussed and

it was proposed to obtain royal permission to rebuild it on the most suitable site on the public plaza, constructing it with the public market on the ground floor and appointed Don Carlos de Reggio . . . and Don Francisco Pascalis de la Barre . . . for the purpose of having such a plan made, which can be attached to the petition that should be made to His Majesty . . .

It is not known if such a plan was ever made, but if it was, it apparently accomplished nothing and the Cabildo devoted its limited funds to repairing the royal jail and restoring the old corps de garde for temporary use as a parish church.

The Cabildo continued to meet in the Government House until the fall of 1791. At its meeting on October 21 that year, it was pointed out that

it was against the . . . laws of the Indies, that the members of the Cabildo hold their sessions at the Government House, as of necessity has been done since the fire in this city during the year 1788, in which most of the houses of the city were destroyed, among them the Cabildo. Noticing the greatest number of houses have been rebuilt, the Commissioners agreed, that in order to comply with the above mentioned law, a comfortable house located in a central place be rented for the purpose of holding the meetings of this Most Illustrious Council until the Cabildo can be rebuilt.

The Commissioners appointed to carry out the resolution were Don Andrés Almonester y Roxas and Don Francisco Pascalis de la Barre, who rented a house on Royal Street [now 812] from a Spanish military officer, Don Manuel Lanzos, for twenty-two pesos per month. On April 1, 1788, only a few days after the fire, Don Manuel had signed a contract with the American builder, Robert Jones, to rebuild his own residence on Dumaine Street [now Madam John's Legacy] and a year later, on April 28, 1789, had contracted with the same builder to construct the Royal Street house. Rental of this house was approved by the Cabildo on November 11, 1791, and it

agreed to inform the city treasurer to supply from city funds whatever is necessary for the payment of the pictures of the King and Queen, ornaments and other things required for the Cabildo.

At the session held a week later, however, Almonester had changed his mind about the Lanzos house and he informed this Most Illustrious Cabildo that, in the house where he resides he has two separate rooms, with a separate staircase from the one leading to his own residence, which rooms he is offering to rent to the Cabildo for its meetings at the rate of ten pesos per month. The Commissioners considering these rooms more suitable for the meetings of the Cabildo than the house they had rented for the purpose, due to its location on the plaza and also that it is a two-story house, agreed to accept said offer . . . and the city treasurer is hereby ordered to pay Don Manuel Lanzos one month's rent for his house.

Two weeks later, on December 2, 1791, after having held at least one meeting in Almonester's house, they decided that the rooms

are very small and are connected with the principal salon of the said house, and the said Royal Ensign [Almonester], offering one large and two small rooms in the same house at the rate of 20 pesos per month, they agreed that these three rooms are more proper for their meetings and accepted the mentioned three rooms for the rental referred to above . . .

All subsequent meetings of the Cabildo were held in Almonester's house, the rent being paid annually until the new Cabildo building was finally completed in 1799.

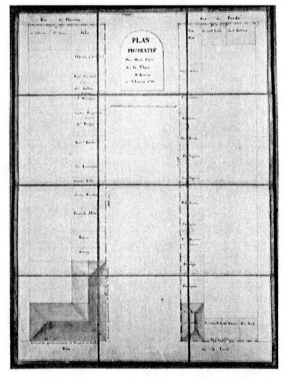

Plan showing the properties amassed by Don Andrés Almonester y Roxas on both sides of the Place d'Armes (1798). The Cabildo met regularly from 1791 to 1799 in Almonester's house, shown here on the corner of St. Peter and Levee (Decatur) streets (lower left).

The New Cabildo (1795-1803)

After the second conflagration, on December 8, 1794, had again practically destroyed the old French corps de garde, the prisons as well as the fire engine house that had been built on the site of the old Cabildo, that Illustrious Body finally decided to take steps to construct for itself a worthy building. Having attended to the most urgent problems of repairing the jail, the Cabildo, at its session on January 16, 1795,

discussed steps to be taken in order to reconstruct the building of this Cabildo which was reduced to ashes during the fire of March 21, 1788 and which never reconstructed, as there were no funds in the city treasury. That office is still not in a position at the present time to handle such expenses and Don

Detail of a lithograph made in 1842 by Jules Lion showing part of the façade of the Cabildo before the addition of the mansard roof.

Richard Koch Collection.

Andrés Almonester y Roxas generously promised that he would reconstruct the Cabildo building, following the same plan he is using in constructing the Presbytère. At the time the building shall have been completed it shall be appraised and its value will be paid out of city funds in installments without detriment to the city treasury nor causing delays in making other payments, to be paid to Almonester whenever it is possible to do so. The Commissioners, grateful for such a generous offer, they accepted it, duly thanking Don Andrés Almonester y Roxas, and they agreed to let this gentleman proceed to reconstruct it under the terms he has proposed, giving him sufficient authority to carry it out.

Soon after the fire of 1788 Almonester had agreed to rebuild the Cathedral and the Presbytère. The plans for both of these structures were drawn by Don Gilberto Guillemard, a Frenchman by birth, who had for many years been in the military service of Spain, having begun his career as a cadet in January 1770. Naturally Guillemard was selected to make the plans for the new Cabildo building. As had been the case with the Presbytère, Guillemard made as much use as possible of the old brick work that still remained on the site after the two great fires. Evidently there were substantial remains of the massive brick walls of the old French corps de garde of the 1750's which could be utilized if the site of the old Cabildo was combined with them, rebuilding both as a single structure having nearly the same frontage to the public square as the new Presbytère.

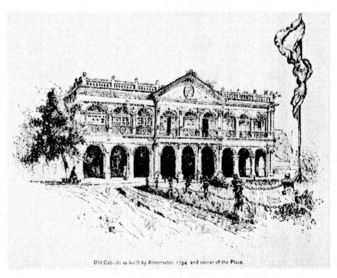

Old Cabildo as built by Almonester, 1794, and corner of the Plaza.

The Cabildo at the time of the Louisiana Purchase. This well-drawn sketch, showing the Spanish arms in the pediment, was the work of the celebrated artist Joseph Pennell who used historical data to bring back the appearance of the building when it was built.

28

At its meeting of November 6, 1795, Governor Carondelet informed the Cabildo that in accepting Almonester's offer to rebuild its building, it had neglected to specify that

> . . . the said Cabildo should extend to the corner of the plaza (to St. Peter Street) including 41 feet front by 60 feet in depth belonging to His Majesty and assigned to quarter the main troops, leaving the lower floor of the building for the same purpose, constructing therein the rooms which might be required for the officer and the soldiers of the guard, the upper floors remaining for the use of this Cabildo forever.

> For this purpose, all the ruins and bricks remaining on the grounds would be left for Don Andrés and besides 2000 pesos would be delivered to him from the royal treasury. The Intendant, with whom His Excellency held a conference about this matter, gave his consent, finding this proposition profitable to the royal interests. It would otherwise be necessary to construct a building in the same place at His Majesty's expense for the use of the said guard. By virtue of this, the Commissioners agreed that the Cabildo will be rebuilt under the terms that have already been stated and that the lower floor of the said space of 41 feet front and 60 feet deep will always be for the use of the said guard; and in view of this, the aforesaid 2000 pesos be delivered to Don Andrés.

Guillemard apparently was greatly influenced in his design of the new Cabildo by the ruined walls of the old corps de garde. Inside, the two long rooms, separated by a heavy wall with five arches, were restored for the use of the corps de garde. The five windows in the old wall along St. Peter Street established the spacing of the windows of the new Council Chamber or *Sala Capitular* which Guillemard designed to occupy the new second floor space above, overlooking the street. Although the fireplace in the lower room was at its Royal Street end, the fireplace in the *Sala Capitular* was placed at the center on the long inner wall of the room. The old mantel was apparently removed when the building was remodeled as a residence for the Marquis de Lafayette during his visit in 1825, it then being considered a clumsy wooden thing, unworthy of the distinguished guest. When first made however, it must have been the best and most elaborate that could be obtained for the room intended to house the sessions of the Most Illustrious Cabildo. The only ones of such elegance surviving from the late 1800's were those from the Bosque House that are now in the State Street residence of Mr. Felix Kuntz who graciously allowed them to be used as a basis for the design of the new one, donated by The Friends of the Cabildo for the restoration of the *Sala Capitular* in 1969.

Although numerous plans have been found for the repairs and additions to the prison buildings back of the new Cabildo, no plans for this most important structure have been located.

Work had been started by December 4, 1795, for on that date the Cabildo "agreed that the hangman could not continue living in the place where he now resides, as it is the place where Don Andrés Almonester has started to build the *Casas Capitulares*." All the work was carried out under Guillemard's supervision and according to his plans, plans based on the ones he had drawn in 1791 for the Presbytère.

Almonester did not neglect seeking royal approbation for all his civic and philanthropic works and finally was honored by the king, being made a Knight of the Royal Order of Carlos III. The ceremonies of the investiture and reception following were described by his contemporary, Joseph Xavier Delfau de Pontalba, whose son was in later years to marry Almonester's daughter Micaëla. Pontalba wrote on September 8, 1796:

> We went this evening to the reception of the famous Knight of Charles III . . . That poor man is never satisfied. As soon.as he gets one thing, he strives for another . . . The reception . . . followed the usual custom. He was enveloped in the great mantle of the Order and his train was carried by three lackeys in red. An immense crowd followed him as he went in state from the Cathedral to his dwelling. He placed himself in his mantle, at the door of his drawing room, where he affectionately kissed on both cheeks all who approached to greet him, to the number of more than three hundred. About eight o'clock in the evening he sent up from the *Place* a balloon accompanied by a small display of fireworks. At the end of a collation consisting entirely of sweet-meats, they played cards until ten o'clock.

Charles IV, King of Spain (1748-1819). It was during his reign that Napoleon forced the retrocession of Louisiana to France. Charles was a great huntsman but a weak monarch.

From a portrait by
Francisco de Goya in the
National Gallery of Art,
Washington.

It must have given Almonester great satisfaction to be the center of so much pomp and ceremony and to parade from the Cathedral he had built, past the new Cabildo, which by then must have been nearing completion on the exterior, to his own residence at the corner of St. Peter and Levee streets, overlooking the river and the public square. This was the large house rented in part for meetings of the Cabildo and the house that he and his family had for a time vacated for the accommodation of Bishop Luis Peñalver y Cárdenas in July 1795 when the new bishop of the newly erected Diocese of Louisiana had arrived from Havana and found the apartments being prepared for his residence in Pontalba's house at the corner of St. Peter and Chartres streets were not completed.

Meanwhile work on the Cabildo continued and periodic payments were made to Almonester as city funds became available. These payments were few and far between. The members of the Cabildo were not unmindful of this, and although Almonester was apparently not extremely popular personally, the Cabildo did recognize his generosity and their indebtness to him, and at their meeting on July 21, 1797, inscribed the following in their minutes:

At this time the Commissioners considering the good deeds done by Don Andrés Almonester y Roxas, Knight of the Distinguished Spanish Royal Order of Carlos III, Colonel of the Battalion of Militia, Commissioner and Royal Ensign, not only to this city, by having built at his own expense the Cathedral, the Chapel of the Convent of the Ursuline Sisters, the Charity Hospital, the hospital of SanLazaro [for lepers], and who at the present time is building the Priest's House made of brick and lime, the first floor being already finished, but also is spending his money freely for the public's benefit. Perhaps by the early part of next year, the Cabildo building will be completed of brick from top to bottom. No doubt its cost will be over 30,000 pesos, without exacting any payment except for this single building, the other buildings having been presented as a gift. The city is only to make partial payments from what is left in the city treasury, after its annual expenses have been covered, to be applied to the appraised value of the property after the said building is completed. This benefit is considered as a great favor as the cash on hand in the city treasury is usually pledged for the public outlays and in case there is a balance left, it is not of a considerable amount. The result therefore will be that several years will elapse before this amount can be paid, the actual benefit being at the present time in favor of this city, and none in favor of the benefactor. Being assured, for these reasons, that we could not have a Cabildo building in this city without having to implore His Majesty's mercy in order to obtain some means for this purpose and as it seems to the Commissioners that the city is anxious to express to the said benefactor in an honorable and creditable manner how grateful we are for said buildings, which is the only thing his modesty would accept, the Commissioners agreed that with city funds, a portrait of the said Don Andrés be made and placed in the Chambers of the Cabildo, with the proper inscription concerning his deeds and liberality.

Don Andrés Almonester y Roxas from a portrait by Salazar.
Courtesy Archdiocese of New Orleans.

A life-size portrait was painted containing such an inscription as called for in the resolution of the Cabildo which is translated as follows:

> Señor Don Andrés de Almonester y Roxas, founder and donor of this Holy Cathedral Church, Knight of the Royal and distinguished Spanish Order of Charles III, Colonel of the Militia of this Plaza, Commissioner and Royal Ensign, in ownership, of the Most Illustrious Cabildo, founder and donor of the Royal Hospital of St. Charles and of its church; founder of the leper's hospital, founder of the church and convent of the Nuns of St. Ursula, founder of the classes for girls to be educated and founder of the Priests House, all of which he built at his expense in this city. The year 1796.

This portrait, now owned by the St. Louis Cathedral, is dated a year prior to the Cabildo's resolution. It is possible that the portrait had actually been completed to commemorate Almonester's investiture in the Order of Charles III, the insigne of which is prominently displayed on his coat, and the Cabildo purchased it or a copy of it to hang in the Council Chamber. The artist was probably Josef de Salazar y Mendoza, a native of Mérida in Yucatan, Mexico, who had come with his wife to New Orleans some years before. He is referred to in Matthias O'Conway's journals in 1789 as "the celebrated, self-taught, portrait painter."

At its meeting of November 10, 1797 a question arose regarding payment to the architect of the new Cabildo. Guillemard, "Lieutenant Colonel of the Royal Army and Commander of the Post" addressed a letter to the Cabildo, the minutes recording that

> by virtue of a resolution of this Cabildo and by orders of El Barón de Carondelet, he made a plan for the construction of the new Cabildo building and that he is, at the present time, directing its construction. He requests that in accordance with the previous promises made to him, certain compensation be assigned to him . . . The attorney Don Manuel Serano stated that in view of the fact that many commissions have been entrusted to the said Commander by this Cabildo without any pay, and since a compensation was verbally offered to him for the plan and supervision of the construction . . . he is of the opinion that, for the time being, he be given 200 pesos as compensation and that if in the future, it is judged that he is worthy of more, same will be taken into consideration.

Don Juan de Castanedo, the Royal Treasurer, whose election as a Commissioner of the Cabildo Almonester had opposed a few months before, opposed the payment to the architect by the city, stating that:

In view of what was contracted with the Royal Ensign [Almonester] concerning the construction of the new Cabildo building, it being stipulated that it is to be built on the same plan as the Presbytère, he is of the opinion that the engineer [architect] who made the plan should not be paid with city funds and that said payment is entirely up to the Royal Ensign.

The Treasurer was overruled and Guillemard was voted the 200 pesos.

Almonester continued to attend to his duties as a member of the Cabildo which included, among other things, the inspection of the almost constant repairs and improvements to the royal jail. On April 3, 1798 he asked for and received from the Cabildo, documents confirming the titles of the lots on the two sides of the *Plaza de Armas* on which in 1850 his daughter Micaëla, Baroness Pontalba, built her notable buildings. At the meeting of April 20, 1798 he presented a long written opinion regarding a chimney tax to pay for street lighting. This was to be his last official act as a member of the Cabildo, for he died suddenly during the following week. On April 25, 1798 he died and was buried in the parish cemetery the following day. On November 11, 1799 his remains were reinterred in the Cathedral he had built.

The day following the funeral, the Cabildo held its regular weekly session and although no official expression of regret was made, Governor Gayoso brought up the problems his death might create in the completion of the Cabildo building. He suggested that Guillemard should be appointed by the Cabildo, to take charge of the work if this was agreeable to the widow. The Cabildo also decided to request the widow "to appoint an expert who together with the said Don Gilberto Guillemard may appraise the work of the Cabildo building in accordance with the progress of the work until this day . . ."

A few weeks later, Almonester's widow, Dona Luisa de la Ronde, requested a payment of 3000 pesos on account of the work. This was refused until the appraisal had been made, the work completed or the king's approval obtained. A payment of 2500 pesos was finally approved on July 27, 1798. Meanwhile Guillemard had been appointed to complete the work but the Cabildo had apparently neglected to authorize a salary for him. At its session on November 9, 1798 a letter from the architect-engineer was presented "stating that he has been appointed to direct and supervise the work of the Cabildo building, in which work he is now engaged and he requests your Lordships to please order that a salary be paid to him for the work out of the city funds, whatever sum your Lordships may find proper." A salary of 300 pesos was approved two weeks later when the Commissioners discussed "the means to be taken in order to finish the Cabildo building without any further delay, which work is being delayed either because certain foremen are delaying the work they have been ordered to execute or because the materials are not being supplied with the required promptness as ordered by Don Gilberto Guillemard." They then approved an additional payment of 3000 pesos to Almonester's widow in an attempt to hasten the work.

At a later meeting Almonester's widow asked to be released from the contract that her late husband had for completing the building. She stated that there were but a few small items to be finished such as the ceilings and staircase and asked that she be allowed to withdraw from the project "leaving the said building in its present unfinished condition." The Cabildo acceded to this request and appointed Don Hilario Boutté and Monsieur Godefroy Dujarreau as experts to appraise the work. Both were prominent architect-builders. They also asked her to name two other experts and stated that the

> said appraisal must comprise the whole building, excluding the actual quarters of the guard . . . and that another appraisal of the upper rooms, built over the *corps de garde* be made so that its separate value be known, so that in case His Majesty refuses to approve the agreement . . . [the widow of] the said Don Andrés Almonester could have the right to make a claim against the party who must pay for the section of that building; that the completion, and direction of the building be entrusted to the Major and Lieutenant Colonel of the Royal Army, Don Gilberto Guillemard; [and] that the 3000 pesos, ordered to be paid to the said lady so that she could finish the said building, be retained . . .

All the correspondence and agreements made between Almonester and the Cabildo were re-examined as well as the royal order approving the agreement. It was finally decided on December 10, 1798 that the appraisal should include the entire new building with the exception of the 41 by 60 foot area on the ground floor occupied by the corps de garde. Only this latter area would be chargeable to the king, the rest of the building, including the *Sala Capitular* and other rooms over it on the second floor, being the responsibility of the Cabildo.

Work continued on the building under Guillemard's direction and it was finally finished sufficiently to be occupied by the Cabildo on May 10, 1799. No special ceremonies seem to have been observed on this historic occasion, but at the bottom of the minutes of the meeting on that day the secretary, Pedro Pedesclaux, made the following notation:

> I certify and give faith that the previous session of the Cabildo was the first session held in the chambers of the new Cabildo building just completed. As evidence, by orders from the Gov-

ernor and President as well as from members who were present at said meeting, I record this fact in the City of New Orleans on May 10, 1799.

The Spanish governor who presided at this historic first session was Don Manuel Gayoso de Lemos, former Spanish governor at Natchez where he had married an American, Elizabeth Watts, in 1792 after the death of his first wife two years before. Unfortunately Elizabeth died only three months after the marriage and Gayoso, about four years later, married her younger sister Margaret Cyrilla Watts by whom he had a son, Fernando. On August 5, 1797 he had appeared before the Cabildo in its rented chambers in Almonester's house, and there took the oath succeeding Carondelet as Governor-General of Louisiana. He was not destined to preside over many sessions of the Cabildo in its new and elegant *Sala Capitular* for on July 28, 1799, scarcely two months after the first session there, Gayoso died suddenly of yellow fever and was buried the next day in the adjacent St. Louis Cathedral.

*Don Manuel Luis Gayoso de Lemos
(1751-1799).*

Litigation over the financial settlement to be made with the widow Almonester continued for several years. On December 30, 1799 she gave her receipt for four months rent of the rooms of her house at twenty pesos per month "from the first of January through the end of April when the Cabildo moved to one of the halls of the *Casa Capitular* which is completed . . ." By the end of June 1800 the appraisal of the new building had not yet been completed and on June 27 the widow urged the Cabildo to see that this was done so that she might complete the accounting of her husband's succession. The treasurer, Castanedo in reply announced "that the experts have already finished their work and have promised daily to furnish the detailed appraisal."

The appraisers, four of the most prominent architects and engineers in the city at the time, finally completed their report and the appraisal in the amount of 32,348 pesos was submitted to the Cabildo at its session on April 9, 1802. The appraisers in turn had to wait until almost the end of the year 1802 to receive an approval of their salaries for their arduous work, after addressing the following appeal to the new governor, Don Manuel de Salcedo:

> Señor Governor-General etc., Don Nicholas Definiels, Juan Maria Dujaro, Bartolome Lafon and Carlos Trudeau with the greatest veneration and due respect present ourselves before Your Lordship and say that in virtue of having been named expert arbitrators on the part of the Illustrious Cabildo and for Mrs. Luisa de Linot, widow of the deceased Colonel Don Andrés de Almonester y Roxas, for the examination, survey, verification and appraisement of the work done on the building, the *Casa Capitular* of this city, which we executed some months ago. A proceeding of this nature requires the greatest precision, minute detail and care whether it be in the survey of each kind of work such as masonry, carpentry, iron work, parts and ornaments of architecture or to examine the hidden materials. For the examination and appraisement of this valuable building we required fifty-two sessions in accordance with the account and sworn statement which we duly present, both in verification of the work as well as our labors in the office sometimes from sunrise until midnight and as we have no other benefits than in our vigilance to merit the public confidence, therefore:
>
> We pray that you deign to order that we be paid our salaries (by those who owe it) according to and in conformity with the regulations drawn up for taxation by His Excellency, Count de O'Reilly. It is mercy that we hope to receive from the justice Your Lordship administers.

On November 20, 1802, Salcedo ordered the city treasurer to make the appropriate payment but the appraisers were not satisfied with the amount of the proposed settlement which was not even offered until February 15, 1803. They complained that they were "allowed eleven reales for each session, a price lower than the wages allowed a day laborer, without considering the more than five months that we were assigned to this matter only, whether it was for different sessions in the Hall of the Illustrious Cabildo with the Commissioner . . . or to consult with the persons more expert on the just price of each part of the work . . . to agree unanimously among ourselves upon the surveys, calculations and appraisement of so complicated a building, and after having finished and drawn up the statement, the Commissioners obliged us to draw up another with more detail and circumstances, with a warning to proceed without delay under penalty (failing in it) to put us in prison with a fine of fifty pesos. From this, we preferred to abandon all rather than to submit to a payment so low and humiliating to our talents and application."

The Governor referred this argument to the original architect of the building, Guillemard, who in a letter of June 3, 1803, supported his fellow professionals, recommending twice as much as had been offered, twenty-two reales for each of the fifty-two sessions or a total of 143 pesos for each of the four experts. The fifty-two sessions were itemized by them as follows:

Namely	*Session*
For the examination of the work previously done to separate it from the new building, one session	1
For examination and survey of the foundation of the work	2
For the survey of the heavy masonry	5
For the survey of the parts and decorations of the architecture	5
For the survey of the carpentry work of the rooms, roofs, staircases, doors and windows, etc.	6
For the investigation of the hidden materials such as lead, iron, etc.	1
For the drawing up of a statement of the work calculations and appraisements of the value of each kind of work required sixteen days from sunrise and many times until 12 o'clock at night	32
	52

There were fifty-two sessions which we swear to have employed faithfully.

Among the more interesting documents presented in these proceeding was the account of Mr. Le Prevost, "sculptor for work of his profession." This included 16 plaster corbels "according to the model" which were placed at the doors opening on the upper gallery. These were done at a cost of 3½ pesos each. For the entrance door, Prevost sculptured "the Arms of this Province, likewise of plaster, according to the model that Our August Sovereign specified . . . for the form—60 pesos." Only one pair of Le Prevost's corbels remained when the restoration

These corbels, sculptured by Cristobal Le Prevost in 1799 to adorn the doorway of one of the Cabildo gallery entrances, survived numerous remodelings. They served as a model for the ornaments over other doorways in the gallery when the Cabildo was restored in 1968-69. (see page 110).

of the Cabildo was begun in 1968, the ones on the end door of the gallery nearest the Cathedral. The others have been restored from these models. Nothing could be found of the Arms of the Province for the entrance door.

By August 19, 1803 a total of 28,000 pesos had been paid to the widow Almonester including 500 pesos paid to Guillemard for her account for his plans and supervision of the work. This left a balance of 4,348 pesos due on the appraised value of the building. This was ordered to be paid at once so that by the time the colony passed from the hands of Spain at the end of the year, the debt owed to Almonester's estate for the construction of this important structure had been fully liquidated.

The records contain little information regarding the furnishings of the new building, but at its meeting on April 3, 1798, the commissioners "discussed the urgent necessity of procuring twelve chairs to be used in the Chambers of this Cabildo, the price of which is 16 pesos 2 reales." The purchase of these chairs was authorized and they were probably used in the new *Sala Capitular*. Other furniture and the portraits of the King and Queen were no doubt moved from the Cabildo's rented rooms in Almonester's house.

Another object of interest that was purchased for the new building and probably was used in the signing of the Louisiana Transfer documents, was a silver writing set. Its purchase was reported by the Treasurer at the Cabildo's session of January 14, 1803 as follows:

> . . . the City Treasurer made known that he was appointed by this Cabildo to provide a writing set of silver, which he bought at a public auction of the estate of the late Governor of this Province, Don Manuel Gayoso de Lemos. It is at present in actual use in this Cabildo and is composed of an inkstand in the shape of a mortar, mounted on its stand, a sand box in the shape of a barrel, a wafer seal in the shape of a drum, another box to hold the quills for the pens and one small bell, all made of silver with the exception of the stand. As all the said pieces were engraved with the coat of arms of the said deceased, those of the city were substituted for them. The whole set cost 84 pesos, which has not been paid.

The payment was immediately authorized, but what eventually became of this historically and artistically priceless object is unknown. This fine writing set was probably placed on the large table that had been especially made for the *Sala Capitular* which, with its cover, had been finished in time for the first meeting in the new building. The master carpenter Urbano Gaignier presented his bill for it in the amount of 22 pesos 1 real which the Cabildo approved during its first session on May 10, 1799. Besides the twelve chairs placed around the table, as previously mentioned, the *Sala Capitular* also contained a number of benches, some of them old ones that had probably been salvaged from the old Cabildo. At the meeting of December 13, 1799 the treasurer reported that "the four benches of this Cabildo are almost all broken and that he had contracted with the blacksmith, Antonio Canne for the repair at 4 reales for each of the 14 braces required to repair them," a total of seven pesos. A few weeks later on January 31, 1800 the treasurer reported that the benches were also "in need of repairs by a carpenter and an upholsterer." A sum of sixteen pesos for the repairs to the four benches was authorized to the carpenter Rafael Bernabe and 18 pesos to the upholsterer Jorge Stillet. From these bits of information contained in the ancient records of the Cabildo, some idea of the furnishings of this historic building can be deduced.

Another important element in the new building was the splendid wrought-iron work of the railings of the upper gallery and the railings in front of the windows of the *sala capitular*. This iron work is perhaps the finest Spanish colonial wrought-iron work to be found in New Orleans, most, if not all of it being from the forges of Marcelino Hernandez. This skillful craftsman was a native of the Canary Islands who had done work for the Orué-Pontalba house (now the Little Theatre.)

Jail Repairs and Additions (1795-1803)

While the new Cabildo building was under construction the seemingly endless work of repairing the royal jail behind it went on. In January 1796 the Chief Constable, Don Francisco Pascalis de la Barre . . .

> presented a petition explaining that, the jail being in his charge, he should live there in conformity with the law that is in force in all the dominions of our Sovereign, to repress the prisoners' abuses, and observe the jailer's good conduct in keeping them safely. For this purpose he would build a house to live in . . . at his own expense in the rear patio of the jail . . . from which several prisoners who had committed grave offenses had escaped from time to time . . .

Permission for the constable's house was granted but it is doubtful that it was ever built. However, housing for the hangman and for some women prisoners had been completed and on March 11, 1796 the builder Domingo Parsigny presented his bill, certified by Guillemard, in the amount of 202 pesos, 4½ reales for the work. Payment for a new sidewalk at the jail was also approved the same day.

A bill of 60 pesos for minor repairs to the jail was paid to Hilaire Boutte in August 1797, and by November of that year it was found that providing quarters for the hangman within the jail had been a mistake. It was noted that "the prisoners in the royal jail are not as safe and secure as they should be. One of them has recently escaped and lately several others also escaped." Apparently the hangman was partly responsible for these escapes and should not be housed within the jail "as there are daily complaints that he introduces alcoholic liquors to the prisoners."

These problems brought about further study and the Cabildo called for a report on "the work most necessary for the safe custody of the prisoners," submitting a detailed plan and its cost. In April 1798 the hangman was dismissed, and a negro slave, Juan Bautista, alias Joe, imprisoned since 1791 for several robberies, was set free and appointed in his place. Finally on June 8, 1798 "they discussed the urgency of repairing the royal jail and agreed to commission Don Gilberto Guillemard to draw up a plan for all the work he might think necessary — not only for the safety of the prisoners but also for their comfort. Whenever Don Gilberto is ready to inspect the said jail, he should be accompanied by the annual Commissioners so that they may agree upon the work to be done there."

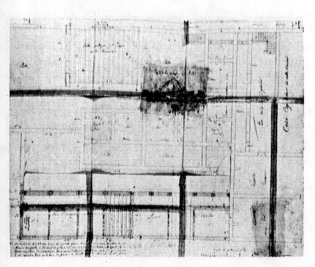

Guillemard's 1799 plan of the new additions to the prison in the rear of the old corps de garde along St. Peter St. Note the plan of the new Cabildo to the right, the plan of the military prison in the center and the plan of the old Criminal Chamber at the upper left.

It was not until January 30, 1799, that Guillemard "produced a plan of the repairs that must be made to the royal jail . . . and the commissioners considering how urgent it is to procure some relief to the inmates, particularly to those detained in the cells, agreed to immediately let out this work on bids . . . repairing the cells, roofing that section close to the yard of the Cabildo and laying bricks in the yard of the royal jail . . ." It was soon realized that the city treasury could not support such an extensive operation at once, so on February 15, 1799 it was agreed that although the proposal should include all of the work "as detailed in the said plan," it should be understood "that the contractor will at once start the work most urgently needed, and successively will continue doing the other work comprised in the plan, based on the funds in the city treasury for the payment of such expenses, until the whole work is finished, as specified in the contract."

The Cabildo moved slowly in getting such work under way; committees studied the project and submitted reports. Finally all the reports were completed, new plans were prepared and submitted on May 10, 1799, at the first meeting held in the new Cabildo building and a week later it was agreed that the contract should be awarded on May 24, nearly a year after this urgent matter had been first discussed. The successful bidder for the contract was Don Juan Maria Godefroi Dujarreau, who by the following October had completed the first phase of the project and had built a room for the hangman which he had already occupied. This room with its chimney had been authorized on August 9, 1799 after the governor informed the Cabildo of the warden's complaint that the hangman, Antonio Sousa drank too much and he was locked up until a house for him could be built "in the patio of the royal jail used by the soldiers."

The principal part of Dujarreau's contract for the jail consisted of a further extension of the building along St. Peter Street behind the jailer's quarters. At the Royal Street end of this extension, on the ground floor, was a kitchen with a large open fireplace. Its chimney extended above the ridge at the center of the gable. Facing the courtyard or patio was an open arcade of four arches. This new addition was two stories in height, a second story also being added over the two rooms and passage of the old jailer's quarters. Seven new cells, with a brick columned gallery facing the patio, were provided by this second story. Each cell had a door and a window opening on to the gallery, with a narrow slit window in each, on the St. Peter Street side, for cross ventilation. The roof had an ample pitch with a slight curve outward at the eaves and was covered with round tiles.

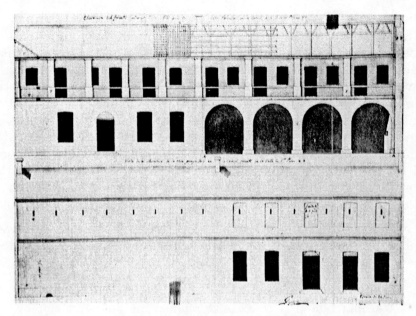

Elevations of the addition to the prison. The elevation facing the patio is shown at the top; the three windows and the door on the first floor to the left are those from the old jailer's quarters behind the corps de garde. The St. Peter Street elevation is shown at the bottom with the old part of the building being at the lower right.

Guillemard's plans for this important addition to the prison have been preserved in the City Archives now at the New Orleans Public Library. These drawings, besides showing the two floor plans of the new prison, also show the plans of the old prison and council chamber, with a detail for a new roof for the latter. It also shows part of the plan of the old corps de garde with part of the plan of the new Cabildo added to it. Indicated as part of Dujarreau's contract were stairways in the narrow courtyard between the new Cabildo and the old French prison of 1730, as well as a new stairway from this prison leading down to the old council chamber facing the church which was at that time being used as a criminal court room. A section through the new prison addition details the tile roof construction, as well as the fireplace and chimney. The drawings also indicate that the partitions between the cells were of brick-between-posts construction. During the recent restoration of the Cabildo, when the plaster was stripped from the wall of the small second floor room between the *Sala Capitular* and the arsenal, the roof line of the old prison could clearly be seen along the arsenal wall, indicating that parts of this building had stood even after the arsenal was constructed in 1839. Most of the old prison, however, was demolished at that time.

On March 7, 1800 Dujarreau informed the Cabildo that he had finished his work on the second part of his contract and was beginning the brickwork and carpentry of the next phase. On May 19 payment of this second installment was approved. Meanwhile the commissioners informed Dujarreau that it wanted real, not simulated, windows or recesses in the St. Peter wall as indicated in Guillemard's plans, these to be set at the height of a man and protected by iron bars to be furnished by a master blacksmith named Juan Dumaine. One such window was ordered for the warden's quarters and one for the kitchen. On November 7, 1800 Dumaine presented his bill for 1,171 pounds of iron "used in making the bars and other work in the royal jail."

By midsummer the jail was not yet completed although well over a year had elapsed since the contract had been awarded. At the meeting of the Cabildo on July 18, 1800 . . .

> the commissioners agreed to notify Don Juan Maria Godfroi Dujarreau to finish without any further delay, the cells in the royal jail, warning him that if by next Monday he does not employ enough laborers to finish the said work, laborers will be employed at his own cost until the same is finished. The commissioners appointed Don Gilberto Andry and Don Jayme Jorda to inspect the finished work as well as that to be finished. It being noticed that in the contract agreed upon with the said Dujarreau, it is not stated that the passageway between the lower cells should be paved with bricks, which it is necessary to do in order to avoid humidity, it was agreed to do so under the same terms as was done in the yard or patio, paying the contractor in proportion to a similar work included in the contract. Likewise it was ordered that the door from the warden's room leading to the patio be condemned and a wall constructed so as to avoid the escaping of prisoners through the gallery of the new building . . .

At the same time it was decided that a brick well with its wooden pump should be built in the patio of the jail for which a new plan was to be prepared and a separate contract let. This was awarded to José Duguet, master mason, who besides building the well and pump, also built "a brass pump-box and a brick tank used by the prisoners for bathing . . . the said Duguet being obligated to guarantee the workmanship of the tank and to correct any defects in case there is any leakage."

On March 13, 1801, Dujarreau reported that he had completed his contract and requested that experts be appointed to inspect it so that he might receive the final payment. Jorda was again appointed to this task, but Gilberto Andry, having resigned from the Cabildo in favor of Don Domingo Bouligny, this latter was appointed in his stead to inspect the work with Jorda. In the meantime the other two members, Pedro de la Roche and Gabriel Fonvergne, reported on new repairs requested by the chief

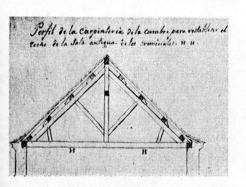

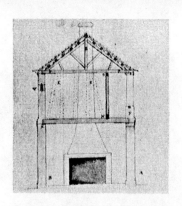

Roof framing for the new roof of the old Council Chamber, or Criminal Chamber.
Drawings by Guillemard, 1799.

Section showing the second story added above the old jailer's quarters.

constable at the jail. These included an additional seven windows in the upper cells facing St. Peter Street as well as various doors, new floors of brick and wood and numerous other repairs to both new and old buildings. Brick work under the supplementary contract was done by Hilaire Boutté who completed his work and requested payment in September 1801. At about the same time Dujarreau also requested the final payment on his contract. As usual, many months were to elapse and many pages of accounts and claims were to be presented, before the account would be settled. Finally on November 11, 1803, almost on the eve of the retrocession of the colony by Spain to France, Governor Salcedo recommended that Dujarreau be paid any accounts still due. Litigation over these accounts probably continued on into the American period before final disposition.

Dujarreau was an able architect and builder and built for himself a fine house on a lot that he bought in 1804 on Royal Street (now 413). This notable house which still stands, was not yet complete when it was sold by the sheriff on July 2, 1808 to satisfy a number of law suits against this unfortunate architect. It eventually came into the possession of Dominique Rouquette whose monogram appears in the balcony railing. Dujarreau's fortunes seemed to go from bad to worse and he was living in two rented rooms on Burgundy Street when on the evening of June 26, 1819, at about the age of seventy-five, "he destroyed himself . . . by throwing himself in the river."

As has been mentioned, parts of his prison building stood until at least 1839 but nothing today remains of this important group of buildings which dated from 1730 to the end of the Spanish Colonial period in 1803. The existing cell blocks in the rear of the Cabildo, although in part on the site of some of these early buildings, are of later construction.

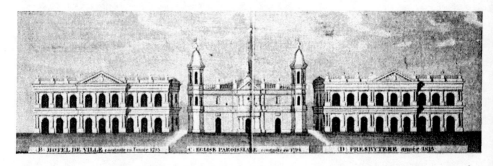

The Cabildo, the St. Louis Cathedral and the Presbytère, marginal sketch from a map by Jacques Tanesse (1817).

Courtesy Richard Koch.

The Cabildo As Seen by Travelers

From the time it was completed in 1799, the Cabildo has always been an object of great interest to the visitor to New Orleans. To many, landing from sailing vessels opposite the public square, it, with the adjacent cathedral and the presbytère, was a major element of one of the first and most dramatic views to be had of New Orleans.

C. C. Robin, visiting the city in 1803, wrote in his *Voyages dans l'interieur de la Louisiane,*

> an entire block was reserved for the *place d'armes,* the one in the middle of the eleven bordering the river. This *place,* fifty toises square, is today embellished at its rear by the regular façade of the cathedral, having on its flanks two other regular edifices; on its right is the city hall, built in a good enough taste; the building on its left is not finished . . . The general appearance of the *place,* with its commercial activity makes a view of it pleasing; it would be an improvement if they had decorated it with trees . . . What is remarkable is that the cathedral, the city hall and the other structures forming the wings were built at the expense of a single Spaniard named Don Andrés Almonester who died only a short while ago, and who had come in poverty to Louisiana. He had besides built the church of the hospital and that of the Ursuline nuns. All of these edifices cost in the neighborhood of two million francs . . . The estate he left was still the greatest fortune in the colony.

A few years later the American Major Amos Stoddard wrote in his *Sketches, Historical and Descriptive, of Louisiana,* published in 1812:

> The cathedral stands at the head of a spacious open square, about four hundred feet from the river . . . The town house is rather an elegant building, two .stories high, and about ninety feet long, with an arched portico, both above and below, along its whole front. The upper arches are glazed, which adds much to the beauty of the structure. The Spaniards occupied one part of the ground story as a guard house, and permitted a notary to

46

occupy the [sic] other as an office. The upper story was appropriated to the use of the cabildo.

In the rear of the town house, and adjoining to it, is the prison. Under the Spanish government it was a wretched receptacle of vice and misery; like the grave it received many tenents [sic], who were soon forgotten by the world: some of them perished with age and disease, and others by the hands of assassins. Criminals, under the sentence of death, were often immured within its walls for years; owing either to the tardiness or lenity of the tribunal at the Havanna, without whose approval no sentence of death could be carried into execution.

When the noted architect, Benjamin Henry Latrobe visited New Orleans in 1819 he remarked, in his *Impressions Respecting New Orleans:*

The public square, which is open to the river, has an admirable general effect, & is intinitely superior to anything in our Atlantic cities as a water view of the city. The square extends along the river about____feet, and is____feet deep. The whole of the side parallel to the river is occupied by the Cathedral in the center & by two symmetrical buildings on each side. That to the West is called the Principal [Cabildo], & contains the public offices & council chamber of the city. That on the East is called the Presbytery . . .

The three most prominent building in the city are the Cathedral, the Principal, and the Presbytère. They form the N.West side of the Place d'Armes. The Cathedral occupies the center; the two others are perfectly symmetrical in their exterior, the Principal to the South, the Presbytère to the North of the Church. Altho' in detail these buildings are as bad as they well can be, their symmetry, & the good proportions and strong relief of the façades of the two latter, & the solid mass of the former produce an admirable effect when seen from the river or the levee.

The construction of these buildings is curious. The foundations are laid about six inches below the natural surface; that is, the turf is shaved off, and logs being then laid level along this shallow trench, very solid piers & thick walls of brick are immediately built upon the logs. The Cathedral is bound together by numerous iron cramps, which appear externally in S and other forms; but I do not think that they were very necessary, the settlement of the buildings here being very equal *in general,* & a few if any cramps appear on the outside of the other two buildings. The SE corner of the Principal, however, has not settled as much as the rest of the front: for tho' no crack appears, the horizontal mouldings are swayed down at least 4 inches towards the NE. The corner that has not settled, as I was informed by the Mayor, was built upon the foundation of an old wall [of the old French corps de garde], from which circumstance it would appear that the earth once pressed down by considerable weight does not afterwards admit of further condensation . . . These three buildings are in fact the best looking in New Orleans at present . . ."

Elevation of the façade of the Cabildo.
Drawing made in 1819 by Benjamin Henry Latrobe.

The town house & Presbytère, the façades of which are exactly alike, are not bad designs en masse, but are bad in detail & execution. The lower story consists of a wide arcade and ranges of rooms behind it; the upper story of a wide gallery, covering also a range of Offices. It is an excellent building for the climate & would be a good one if judiciously warmed for one more northerly.

The effect of the front at a distance is imposing, & the deep recesses and bold dimensions of the arches give it a light as well as magnificent appearance . . .

In respect to the slaves commited to jail in New Orleans, & employed in the public work, I cannot say that they are hard worked. The clanking of their chains, which being fixed around the ankle are brought up along the leg and fastened to the waist, is a distressing sound . . . They are now employed in leveling the dirt in the unpaved & cut up streets, in making stages from the levee to the ships in the harbor, & other works of mere labor, about which they seem to go very much at their leisure.

One morning while attending the Council at the Principal, or town house, I was excessively annoyed for nearly an hour by hearing successive cracks of a whip, each followed by a scream, and as the tone of the screams varied, I presumed it was a day of execution at the jail, which is behind the Principal.

Latrobe made a rough sketch plan of the Cabildo, evidently from memory because of obvious discrepancies in proportion and in the number of offices indicated. It does however, indicate the location of the principal rooms and shows that the grand staircase existed then as it does now. Evidence was found, however, in the restoration of the 1960's that the stairway may have

48

originally been intended as an exterior one on the gallery but was moved to the interior after the second-story walls were completed. An early plan of the Presbytère in the Spanish archives, dated about 1789, indicates such an exterior stair location on that building. Latrobe also made a rather careful elevation drawing of the Cabildo showing a garlanded oval in the pediment that had evidently originally contained the Spanish coat of arms.

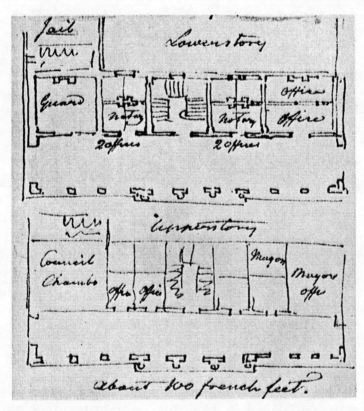

Rough sketch of plans of the Cabildo by Benjamin Henry Latrobe (1819).

A few years later Paxton's *Notes on New Orleans* appeared in his 1822 City Directory, saying of the Cabildo only that:

> On one side of the church is the City Hall and on the other the Presbytere, two buildings with handsome and uniform fronts: these are situated on Chartres street, opposite the elegant public square called "The Place of Arms," occupying the whole front between St. Peter and St. Ann streets and forming together a very handsome and pleasing aspect, particularly from the Levée, where they can be seen to the greatest advantage.

John H. B. Latrobe, son of the noted architect Benjamin H. B. Latrobe, who visited New Orleans in 1834, wrote:

> After pursuing *La Rue de la Levee* until I came to the public square, I crossed it and had before me the Cathedral, the Calaboose and the building in which the Courts are held. The Cathedral is a venerable looking building, for time and the climate have quite discolored the plaster with which its walls are covered . . .The Calaboose and court house are on either side of it, match each other, and with the Cathedral, exhibit to the *coup d'oeil* quite an imposing aggregate of law, religion and punishment . . .
>
> There is a police here in uniform called the City Guard. I met several of them in the market this morning in a blue cloth dress— single breasted coat with white metal buttons and a sword fastened to a black leather belt over the shoulders. A dowdy uniform upon a dowdy looking set of fellows.

The Cabildo, the St. Louis Cathedral and the Presbytère.
From "Gibson's Historical Epitome
of the State of Louisiana with an
historical notice of New Orleans". (1840).

In Gibson's *Guide and Directory of Louisiana, New Orleans and Lafayette,* published in 1838, the Cabildo together with the Presbytère and the Cathedral are described as the —

Public Buildings
Fronting on the Place d'Armes, or Parade Square
These are three in number : —

The chief is that in the center which bears the name of the Cathedral, or Church of St. Louis . . .

The front of the building [the Presbytère] on the right of the Cathedral looking from the Public Square towards it, is in the lower story of the Tuscan order with a wide portico along the front of the edifice supported by antae between semi-circular arches, of which four in the middle are strengthened in front by Tuscan columns, and those at the angles by two clustered pilasters . . .

The front of the upper story is of the Ionic order, but generally similar to the lower. The entablature is submounted by a denticulated cornice, and the pediment is relieved by an oblong shield. The building on the left [the Cabildo] is in all general respects the same as what we have just described except that the main entrance under the portico is of the Tuscan order, and that the stair within is a winding one, leading to the upper story by three flights; also that the pediment of the front bears the American Eagle with a cannon and piles of balls — the instruments to retaliate and destroy; as that in the other edifice bears the shield to defend.

The lower story contains the City Guard room, Calaboose or Police Prison and that above, the office of the Mayor, the City Treasurer and the Comptroller, and also the room for the meeting of the City Council.

In more recent years, around 1930, the architectural historian Thomas T. Tallmadge wrote in his *Story of Architecture in America:*

The famous Cabildo, flanking with its counterpart the Cathedral, is much more provincial. With all its charm, the proportions of the Cabildo are heavy and the mouldings coarse. It shows its Spanish ancestry, but it is not the elaborately ornamented Churrigueresque that we found in California Missions. It is rather of the Graeco-Roman type of Herrara and the Spanish Classicists, and even at that the influence of French environment is plainly discernible. The charming wrought iron balconies, erected in 1795, are French, as is the general disposition and or orderliness of the composition. The high roof with its unusual dormer windows we are told was added in 1851, though it appears to be a part of the original design. In the Salle Capitulaire, the great audience hall took place the ceremonies of the transfer of the Louisiana Territory, first from Spain to France and afterwards from France to the United States.

Gayoso's Coat of Arms.

Raising the American Flag in front of the Cabildo on December 20, 1803.
From the painting by Thule de Thulstrup.
Courtesy Louisiana Historical Society
and the Louisiana State Museum.

M. Laussat Turns Over Louisiana to the United States (1803)

In the winter of 1803, Pierre Clément de Laussat, the French colonial prefect and commissioner sent to Louisiana by Napoleon to take over the colony from Spain, was one of the principal actors in the drama which ended in his handing the territory to the United States. Within twenty days the action of the formal cession from Spain to France and from France to the United States took place in the *sala capitular* of the Cabildo. Laussat's journal vividly paints a picture of these events. Of the transfer from Spain to France he wrote:

> At 11:45 on November 30, 1803, I set afoot for the City Hall [the Cabildo], escorted by about sixty Frenchmen. The brig *L'Argo* fired a salute as we went past. We arrived at the Place [d'Armes]. The crowd was already considerable. The Spanish troops were lined under arms on one side and the militia on the other. The drums rolled before the guardhouse as I passed. The commissioners of His Catholic Majesty came to meet me halfway down the room. Monsieur de Salcedo [the Spanish governor] seated himself in the middle of an armchair; I sat in another on his right, the Monsieur the Marquis de Casa-Calvo on his left. I presented my powers and the order of the king of Spain. The secretary, Don Andrés López de Armesto, was ordered to read the credentials of his nation's commissioners, and at my command, Daugerot, clerk of the marine, read my own powers.
>
> The Marquis de Casa-Calvo declared in a loud voice that "the subjects who did not wish to remain under Spanish domination were from that moment completely freed of their oath of allegiance." The governor, at the same time, handed me on a silver tray the keys to forts St. Charles and St. Louis. He then gave up his seat and I took it myself.
>
> Don Andrés forthwith read in Spanish the *procès-verbal* agreed upon and transcribed in advance of the cession, and Daugerot immediately afterwards read the French version.
>
> We signed and affixed our seals.
>
> We then arose and went out on the balconies of the City Hall.
>
> When we appeared, the Spanish flag which was flying on the pole was lowered and the French flag was hoisted.

Laussat gave a sumptuous party the next afternoon, inviting seventy-five people, Spanish, American and French, for dinner. At nightfall they were joined by more than a hundred ladies and gentlemen, and dancing began. A supper was served at three o'clock in the morning and gambling, which had begun at dinner time, continued until eight, although the last of the dancers had gone home an hour before!

Louisiana was again under French rule for just twenty days. During this short interregnum Laussat set up a city council which held meetings, selected a mayor, and organized a company of militia, many of whom were native Frenchmen. He then pre-

Napoleon Bonaparte (1769-1821) First Consul of France, had succeeded in getting Spain to retrocede Louisiana to France under the secret treaty of San Ildefonso (1800). Expeditions to take possession of the colony were organized, but yellow fever and the Negro uprisings in Saint-Domingue and a winter of great cold forced Napoleon to abandon his plans.

From a painting by Baron François Pascal Simon Gérard, executed in 1803, the year of the Louisiana Purchase.

pared to turn the territory over to the Americans. The fateful day was to be December 20, 1803, a fine clear, mild day,. and again Laussat made his way from the Marigny mansion, which served as the prefecture during his New Orleans stay, to the Place d'Armes, this time to cede Louisiana from France to the United States. He wrote:

> The pretty women and the dandies of the town filled the balconies overlooking the square. The Spanish officers stood out in the crowds because of their feathered hats. At none of the previous ceremonies had there been such a large attendance by the curious. The eleven galleries of the City Hall were full of beautiful ladies.
>
> The American troops . . . arrived in platoons to the beat of drums, marching along the river to the square and, facing the militiamen, who had their backs to the City Hall, they assumed battle formation.
>
> The commissioners, Messieurs Claiborne and Wilkinson, were received at the foot of the stairs of the City Hall by the battalion chief, Vinache, the major of the militia, Livaudais, and the secretary of the French commission, Daugerot. I advanced toward them, midway down the length of the council room. Claiborne seated himself in an armchair at my right, and Wilkinson in another at my left. I announced the purpose of the ceremony. The commissioners presented their powers to me, their secretary reading these in a loud voice. Immediately afterward, I ordered to

So intent was Napoleon on occupying Louisiana that he sent Pierre-Clément Laussat to New Orleans as a Colonial Prefect to prepare for the arrival of the French troops.

From a portrait by Jean-François-Gille Colson.

Laussat's Stamp as Prefect

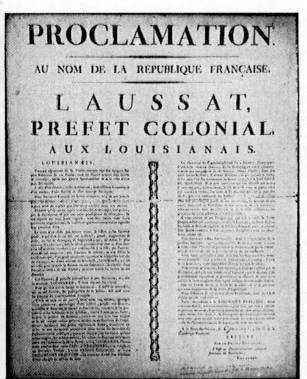

Laussat arrived in New Orleans in March, 1803 to receive the transfer of the colony from the Spanish officials. On March 26, Laussat published a "Proclamation in the name of the French Republic." To a large extent, the Creole population, although predominantly French in origin, language and customs, faced the prospect of the change in regime with little enthusiasm.

Louisiana State Museum.

This was New Orleans at the time of the transfer of Louisiana in 1803. Painted by J. L. Bouqueto de Woiseri, the view was made from the handsome house of the Marigny family which was situated at the foot of Elysian Fields Avenue and in which Laussat resided in New Orleans.

Courtesy Chicago Historical Society.

in the Place d'Armes before the Cabildo, the French flag was lowered and the American flag raised. It was reported that the American flag stuck while being raised. The spectators remained silent and motionless except for a crowd of Americans who waved their hats and shouted "hurrah."

From a painting by Henry Hintermeister
in the Louisiana State Museum.

William C. C. Claiborne, United States Commissioner who signed the procès verbal" at the Cabildo which transferred Louisiana to the United States. Claiborne was appointed governor and after statehood was elected to the office by popular vote.

*From an engraving by
J. B. Longacre from
a miniature by A. Duval.*

General James Wilkinson, who commanded the American troops sent to receive Louisiana, was the other commissioner who signed the "procès verbal" at the Cabildo.

*From a miniature, courtesy
Hugh M. Wilkinson, Sr.*

be read: first, the treaty covering the cession; second, my powers; and third, the act covering the exchange of ratifications. I then declared that I transferred the country to the United States . . . I handed the keys of the city, interlaced with tricolor ribbons, to Monsieur Wilkinson, and I immediately released from their oath of fidelity to France all those inhabitants who wished to remain under the domination of the United States.

The *procès-verbal* was read, first in French by Daugerot, then in English by Wadsworth.

Both sides signed alternately with their respective secretaries. We then went to the main balcony of the City Hall. As soon as we appeared the French standard was hauled down; the American standard was hauled up: they were both stopped then at the same height. A cannon shot gave the signal for salvos from the forts and the batteries.

Laussat was touched by the devotion of the militiamen, and when the officers approached him to say farewell while still wearing their tricolor cockades, he fled to his office deeply moved.

The Frenchman gave another magnificent dinner and soiree, with dancing and gambling (including craps). He wrote that all the society of the colony took part with toasts drunk to the roar of cannon, ending his description with:

For a certainty, the banks of the Mississippi had never before seen an assemblage or fete as resplendent and as animated as this one.

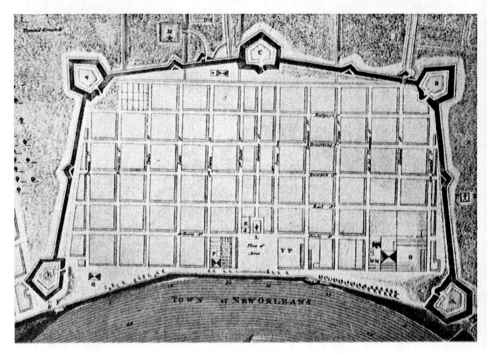

Plan of New Orleans as it was in 1803 by J. L. Bouqueto de Woieserie.

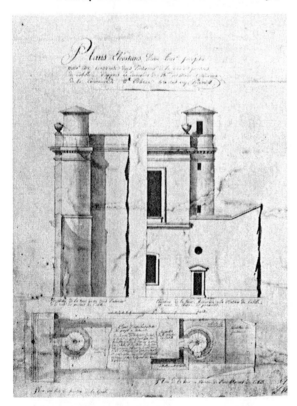

Plan of a turret to contain a circular stairway to provide access to the roof of the Cabildo (1807). (see page 62).

Hyacinthe Laclotte,
Architect.

The City Hall (1803-1853)

The Place d'Armes in 1803. This drawing by J. L. Bouqueto de Woiseri, was made at the time of the Louisiana Purchase. It shows the Cabildo, the St. Louis Cathedral and the half-finished Presbytère with the military parade ground which was the Place d'Armes. At this time the square was flanked by "very extensive brick stores," the property of Don Andrés Almonester y Roxas. It was here that the flag ceremony of December 20, 1803, took place.

In 1804 the coat of arms of the Spanish crown still embellished the pediment of the Cabildo. In a burst of patriotic fervor, the city council decided to have it removed before the July 4 celebration of that year. A sculptor named Le Prevost was employed to create substitute "armorial bearings" and when he had them almost finished in 1806 the council decided to suspend the work until it could make up its mind whether to place a clock on the front of the City Hall. Two years later they were still debating the placing of the clock, and it was not until 1819 that the council agreed to share the expense of erecting a central tower on the Cathedral next door and installing a Paris-made clock in it. The matter of the pediment apparently dragged on for fifteen years.

In 1821 the council made a contract with the talented Roman sculptor Pietro Cardelli who had done work on the Capitol in Washington and who had probably come to New Orleans at the suggestion of the architect Benjamin Latrobe, who had designed the city's first waterworks. The contract called for:

"An eagle, placed in the center of trophies of arms, flags, etc., entirely similar, in close proportion to the model and sketch which he had deposited with the City Council. The work will be modeled in clay, of the width and the height of the pediment of the City Hall where it is to be placed . . . The said work will be afterwards molded in plaster of Paris and solidly fixed to the said pediment. There it shall be hardened with boiling oil and the whole will be painted to simulate white marble."

The pediment of the Cabildo showing the sculpture created by Pietro Cardelli in 1821.
Photograph by Ray Cresson.

Cardelli's contract price was $390, but the council was so pleased with his work that they appropriated another $100 for him as a token of their satisfaction. Cardelli stayed in New Orleans and died there in 1822; his work, still ornamenting the pediment of the Cabildo after nearly a century and a half, is an enduring monument to his skill.

In February 1805, the Louisiana Territorial Council furnished the city with a charter. Containing nineteen sections, this document defined the city's boundaries, named its officers of mayor, recorder, fourteen aldermen, treasurer and subordinate officers. The aldermen were to compose the city council and the charter gave the mayor and council, acting together, the right to tax all real and personal property and to carry on the various functions of a municipality.

On March 11, 1805, the new council was installed in the *sala capitular* (now to serve as the council chamber) with some pomp. Governor Claiborne, accompanied by various military and civil authorities and many citizens, arrived at midday. The governor proclaimed James Pitot, who had previously filled the office, as mayor; Dr. John Watkins was sworn in as recorder (assessor) and the first city council, composed of Felix Arnaud, James Garrick, Joseph Faurie, François Duplantier, P. Lavergne, J. B. Macarty, F. K. Dorville, Thomas Porée, François Guérin, Guy Dreux, Pierre Bertonière, Antoine Argotte, and Thomas Harman (one member, Bellechasse, was not present) took the oath of office. At the close of this ceremony Mayor Pitot made a short address, after which he, Governor Claiborne and the citizens present retired and the council held its initial meeting, the first

The first mayor of New Orleans was appointed by Laussat during the short interval that he governed after the end of the Spanish regime. He was Etienne Boré, the New Orleans planter who is credited with being the first in Louisiana to have produced sugar in commercial quantities. *Etienne Boré (1741-1819) from a portrait that once hung in the New Orleans Sugar Exchange.*

James Pitot (1761-1831) was elected mayor of New Orleans by the municipal council in 1804 after the resignation of Etienne Boré, and was subsequently appointed mayor by Governor Claiborne under the new charter of 1805.

From a miniature, courtesy of René J. Le Gardeur, Jr.

of many which would be held in this chamber for nearly fifty years.

Prior to the Louisiana Purchase, the official religion of the colony was Roman Catholic, and public Protestant worship was forbidden. After 1803 there was full religious freedom, but no Protestant church, and the influx of Americans, most of whom were Protestant, soon caused three of them — James M. Bradford, James C. Williamson and Edward Livingston — to write to Episcopalian Bishop Benjamin Moore of New York to send them a minister. The young man who answered the call was the Reverend Philander Chase, and on his arrival in the city he preached the first sermon to an organized Protestant congregation in the whole of the vast Louisiana Territory. The place: the Cabildo. The date: November 1, 1805. This was the beginning of Christ Church (Episcopal), a congregation which is still flourishing today and the seat of the bishop of the Episcopalian diocese of Louisiana.

From the time of the transfer of the Louisiana Territory (December 20, 1803) a detachment of regular United States troops had been stationed in the lower floor of the Cabildo where they were on duty day and night. When the mayor approached the City Hall each day there was a ruffle of drums and the soldiers lined up in two ranks before the entrance and presented arms as His Honor passed them. At Mayor Watkins's request, Claiborne withdrew the troops in August 1805 and quartered them in barracks. The lower floor of the Cabildo was then occupied by the gendarmerie (police) whose officers had initiated the request for the quarters. The picturesque ceremony was continued, however, with the police doing the saluting instead of the troops, and this went on until Mayor Freret's time (1840's). Freret considered the parade a holdover from Spanish colonial times, useless and a little absurd, and he directed its discontinuance, for which he was warmly praised in the newspapers.

By 1806 the Cabildo, besides housing the mayor and the city council, was the domicile of the superior court and of its clerk, of the county judge and of the notary Pierre Pedesclaux, who had an office on the ground floor. The prison at the rear of the building was a constant nuisance to the council who could hear the cries of prisoners being chastised and smell the fetid odors coming from it. In addition, the jailer, who was apparently using the yard and some of the cells to raise chickens and pigs, was expressly forbidden to do so and ordered to keep the courtyard clean.

The ever-present danger of fire caused the council on January 31, 1807, to pass an important fire ordinance. This was the famous "Bucket Ordinance" by the terms of which each householder was required to keep two buckets in readiness. Among the other stipulations, Article XXII read:

"There shall be constantly in one of the halls of the City Hall, under the peristyle, a depot of four engines, with twelve dozen buckets, twelve ladders, ten grappling irons and their chains, ten gaffs, twelve shovels, twelve pickaxes and ten sledgehammers, all with the mark of the city . . . Above the door there shall read in large letters in the English and French languages — "DEPOT DES POMPES" . . ."

There was to be a watchman on the roof of the City Hall who was to ring a bell at the cry of fire, and the problem of providing access to the roof of the building occupied the council for several months. Perhaps the necessity for action was hastened by the fact that on March 4, 1807 the Cabildo itself had a narrow escape from destruction by fire. Sparks from the open fireplace in the room occupied by the Superior Court ignited the floor, but thanks to the quick action of a guard the blaze was extinguished before much damage was done. After several plans had been suggested, one of them, a turret to contain a circular staircase designed by the architect Hyacinthe Laclotte, was approved by the council. This interesting plan called for the stairway to be added to a far corner of the Cabildo with a door leading into the street next to the church. The city fathers found Laclotte's plan too expensive to execute and his turret was never built.

The Place d'Armes looked like this in 1845. The Cabildo, Cathedral and Presbytère form an impressive background for the soldiers about to execute a military drill. From a Lithograph by Thomas Williams.

His meticulous drawing still exists and from it we have a detailed view of part of the side of the Cabildo as it was in 1807.

In 1806 the gendarmerie was disbanded by the city council and a new police system inaugurated. The officers of the gendarmes had stabled their horses in a building adjoining the City Hall and the council rented the stables for $50 a month to one William James. One of the stipulations of the contract was that James agreed "not to deposit hay or straw in the loft over the said stables, but to keep the same in the brick building in the courtyard," because of the danger of fire. Another danger from fire — and it was a wonder the Cabildo did not burn down — was the storage of oil for lighting the street lamps in it. In 1821 the city's primitive street lights were strung across intersections between two poles and the oil to light them was stored in "cisterns" in the rear of the City Hall. To compound the danger, the oil vats were right next to a structure housing the arsenal!

On September 23, 1809, the Charity Hospital, which had been a gift to the city by Don Andrés Almonester y Roxas in 1786, burned with a loss of four lives. Mayor James Mather thereupon turned the upper gallery of the City Hall into an emergency hospital and brought thirty patients who had been evacuated from the burned buildings there until they could be transferred later to the plantation home of a Madame Jourdan below the city where a temporary hospital was set up.

A happier use of the upper gallery was made in the 1830's when the council permitted the Grenadiers and other companies of the Louisiana Legion to use it as a banquet hall. In 1830 and 1831, the anniversary of the Battle of New Orleans was celebrated by the Grenadiers on January 8 in this historic spot.

In 1836 the City Council decided to enlarge the *sala capitular*. A resolution passed on April 9 of that year called for the removal of the wall separating that chamber from part of the gallery and extending the length of the room to accommodate "in a suitable manner, all the members of said general council". The council secretary was also instructed to provide an additional chandelier.

Through the years the Cabildo housed several libraries. The New Orleans Library Association, created by an act of legislature in 1805, had by 1810 accumulated a fair library. For several years the library was housed in one of the rooms of the State House on Decatur Street, but when the corner room on the lower floor of the Cabildo next to the Cathedral became vacant in 1818 the Library Association asked for and received permission to move its 3,000 books into it. They had hardly been installed in 1819 when the city council changed its mind and ordered the Library Association to move its books back to the State House — they needed the room "for quartering the militia whenever they are on active duty to watch the city"

The Law [later Louisiana Bar] Association, which had been formed in 1847, had its library "in one end of the hall" of the Cabildo. In 1854, the Association complained to the City Council that it needed larger quarters and that the roof leaked, damaging its books. This library, which had grown to 12,000 volumes in 1899, was housed in the Cabildo until 1910, when it was moved to the Civil Courts building on Royal Street at the time that the Supreme Court left the Cabildo.

Beginning in 1857, the Cabildo housed a public school library. An ordinance passed on July 31, 1857, turned over to the public school system of the Second (School) District a room (probably one on the third floor) "now occupied as an arsenal by several military companies" and the military was relegated to a room formerly occupied by a recorder. The public school library in the Cabildo was much smaller than that in the new city hall on St. Charles Street. The latter contained some 12,000 books and pupils could borrow books on payment of 25¢ a month. The Cabildo library contained only 4,000 volumes, but it was open to the public although books could not be removed from the building.

After the departure of the Supreme Court and the conversion of the Cabildo into the Louisiana State Museum, a top floor room was used to house the reference library of the museum and that of the Louisiana Historical Society. The museum library was moved to its present quarters at St. Ann and Chartres Streets (the Lower Pontalba Buildings) in 1930.

The flat roof of the Cabildo, like the flat roofs of other Spanish New Orleans buildings, was never very satisfactory. Soon after the transfer of the territory, Mayor Pitot inspected the terrace, and the council ordered the roof to be "cemented all around, sanded and tarred." In 1818, there were more leaks and more repairs needed, and this problem persisted until the mansard roof was added in 1847.

In January of that year the Cabildo was "leaking everywhere" and something had to be done. The city had grown and more room was needed in the City Hall. The year before, Baroness Pontalba of Paris, the owner of the buildings on each side of the Place d'Armes, had submitted plans which had been made under her personal direction, probably in Paris, which contemplated the construction of a two-story façade in front of her old buildings, thus extending the arcades like those of the Cabildo and the Presbytère buildings along two sides of the square. This would have given the square a character similar to that of the public gardens of the Palais Royal, the Place des Vosges and the Rue de Rivoli in Paris. In return, she asked for two feet of land which would be taken from either side of the square so as not to reduce the width of the street, and also that she be relieved from paying city taxes on her buildings for twenty years.

At the time this proposal came up, the authorities of the Second Municipality were building James Gallier's classic City Hall and there was strong rivalry between the two sections of the city. An opportunity to improve the very heart of the First Municipality by such a dramatic change was too good to be passed up even though there was to be a tax concession. The council complied with all of the Baroness's requests.

The Baroness's plans were to be kept in the city archives for it was "well understood that the whole façade of the said construction on St. Peter Street and St. Ann Street will be executed an all points according to the plan submitted." Unfortunately, these plans have disappeared from the city archives, but the design of the façades of the Baroness's buildings very probably included mansard roofs and dormer windows. Undoubtedly the Baroness's designs influenced Louis Surgi, city surveyor, in the design of the mansard roof with dormers for the Cabildo which was accepted by the council. In fact, the council was so impressed with Surgi's addition that it urged the wardens of the Cathedral who owned the Presbytère, which was then serving as a courthouse, to improve their building "on the same style and plan with the City Hall." J. P. Butterly was the successful bidder for the work on the Cabildo with a contract price of $5,150.

Jackson Square in 1858. The Cabildo and the Presbytère have had mansard roofs added; the St. Louis Cathedral has been rebuilt and the monument to General Andrew Jackson, surrounded by a fine garden in the French style, is flanked on both sides by the newly constructed Pontalba Buildings. Woodcut from Ballou's Pictorial, April 24, 1858.

Butterly set to work to remove the old roof, and a writer in the *New Orleans Weekly Delta* of June 7, 1847, noted the demolition with some regret:

> They have commenced to tear down the terrace over the building occupied by the Mayor and Recorder Genois. The little green shrubs that were growing on the top of the venerable building and gave it an ancient and monastic look, and the venerable grey plaster and time-honored bricks have been hurled to the ground by the Titans at work on the roof . . . In a little while, however, the improvements will be completed and the old Calaboose [which is what the Cabildo was called in those days because of the prison in the rear] like a man with a new hat, will come out with a brand new "tile" [1847 slang for a high hat].

Butterly, however, did not do the work on the new roof in such a way as to please the engineer Surgi, and he was eventually fired from the job, the work being completed by Maurice Oulif.

When the new third story, with its mansard roof and dormers, was nearing completion, the *Delta's* observer philosophized:

> The venerable old building opposite the Place d'Armes, yclept, the Calaboose, is being renovated to such an extent that it will be scarcely known by those who have been absent from the city for a year . . . The necessity for the renovation of this antiquated pile, is a forceable illustration of the progress of time. If the old building could speak, what stories it could tell of Spanish Dons, gallant Chevaliers from France, lovely ladies, and others who, years and years ago have been laid in their silent tombs! Thus it is — the old time wearing away for the advance of the future — old customs have to give place to the innovations of the present — and the old Calaboose, that had stood the storms of more than half a century, is now surmounted with roof and windows like those of an old Virginia mansion! "So runs the world away!" Grass grows upon the graves, and over the monuments of the past we build emblems of the future!

> — *New Orleans Weekly Delta*, January 17, 1848.

In 1850, the council decided further to embellish their City Hall. The outside of the Cabildo was finished in brown stucco which "had the appearance of stone" and the *Daily Picayune* reported that similar treatment was planned for the Presbytère.

An ordinance was passed to pave the entrance hall with marble tiles, paint the walls to imitate marble, and have new entrance doors made. These wrought-iron gates, still in use, are one of the most attractive features of the old building. They were made by the skilled firm of Pelanne Brothers after the design of Louis Pilié, city surveyor, and an observor in the *Louisiana Courier*, passing by in March, 1851, after the new gates had been installed, praised them highly:

Gate of the City Hall

We noticed in passing in front of the City Hall, a magnificent iron gate recently set. It is a work of art executed by the Pelanne brothers, blacksmiths of the Municipality, on the design of Mr. L. Pilié, surveyor.

The design is elegant, well studied. The Pelanne brothers have translated it into wrought iron. All the pieces are admirably adjusted. It would be difficult to unite more solidity and more elegance in form to more finish in execution.

The massive wrought-iron gates of the Cabildo are splendid examples of the iron work of the 1850's for which New Orleans has long been noted.

Photograph by Jack Beech.

A souvenir of the divided municipalities — a $200.00 bond of the First Municipality. This well-engraved certificate had for its central illustration a view of the Place d'Armes. Issued in 1837, it bore 6% interest. It was engraved by the New Orleans engraver John V. Childs.

For sixteen years — between 1836 and 1852 — the city of New Orleans was governed by a curious charter which divided the city into three municipalities under a single mayor. The division had come about because of friction between the Creoles and the Americans. Under a charter which provided for recorders and councils for each municipality, each section had full tax administration, public improvement power and a separate police force. The First Municipality was basically the Creole Vieux Carré, from Canal to Esplanade and from the river to the lake. The Second, which had been largely developed by the American element after the Louisiana Purchase, extended from Canal Street to Felicity Street and from the river to the lake. The Third Municipality extended below the First Municipality to the shores of Lake Borgne. The council of the First Municipality remained in the Cabildo and the Second Municipality council leased a building on the corner of St. Charles and Lafayette streets opposite the present Gallier Hall as a municipal hall.

By 1850, the impracticability of this arrangement was all too apparent, and an act was introduced and passed in the state legislature to consolidate the three municipalities and also annex the suburb of Lafayette. The new city charter was signed by the governor on February 23, 1852. It was during this period that City Hall (now Gallier Hall) was erected as the municipal hall for the second district. An element in the city government urged that the glittering new building on Lafayette Square be made headquarters for the entire city government, but the editor of *The Daily Delta* urged caution, writing on March 31, 1852:

For more than a hundred years [*sic*] that old building [the Cabildo] has been the seat of our city government. Here assembled, in turn, our city legislators under three different nationalities. Over that antique building was waved the proud banner of Castile and Aragon, the tri-color of France, and the stars and stripes of the United States. It is associated with many proud and dear recollections, and is enshrined in the hearts and memories of our old population, by ties which cannot be broken without producing many a pang . . .

The editor proved to be a sentimentalist; the consolidated city government moved into its proud new building which was dedicated on May 10, 1853, and the Cabildo lost its chief tenant.

Joseph Pennell visited New Orleans to make illustrations for a magazine. This drawing, the original of which is now in the Louisiana State Museum, he titled "The Cabildo Today 1890".

The ornate *"Arc de Triomphe"* erected in the *Place d'Armes* for Lafayette's visit was designed by the city's engineer, J. Pilié and made by J. B. Fogliardi, who also made this engraving of it. It was 68 feet high, 58 feet wide and 25 feet deep. The top of the arch was 40 feet above the street. It was probably constructed of canvas over a wooden framework; the base was painted to resemble green marble and the top portion yellow marble. Painted on the base were figures representing Justice and Liberty; adorning the arch were two allegorical forms depicting Fame with trumpets and ribands bearing the names Washington and Lafayette. The roof bore inscriptions in French and English, "A grateful Republic consecrates this monument to Lafayette." The topmost figure was that representing Wisdom crowning a bust of Franklin.

An interesting sidelight on the design of the arch and the general decoration of the city for Lafayette's visit was that the City Council was so pleased with Pilié's work that they voted him a $400.00 bonus!

From *"Visite du General La Fayette a la Louisiana"*, 1825.

70

General Lafayette Slept Here (1825)

A celebration that the city never forgot came in 1825 when sixty-eight-year-old General Lafayette, hero of the American Revolution, on a tour of the United States, accepted the invitation of New Orleans to visit the Crescent City. Shortly after the departure of the distinguished guest, "R.P." a citizen of New Orleans, published a flowery little book entitled *The Visit of General Lafayette in Louisiana,* in which he described the visit in great detail. Some excerpts:

Marie-Joseph-Paul-Yves-Roch-Gilbert du Motier, Marquis de Lafayette (1757-1834).

Drawn by Julien, lithographed by Bichebois a few years after his visit to New Orleans.

A committee on arrangements, presided by the Governor was organized. It was composed of Governor Johnson, Messrs. Villeré, Morgan and Duplantier on the part of the State: of Mr. Roffignac, Mayor, Mr. Prieur, Recorder, and Aldermen Christy, Cox and Davezac, for the City of New Orleans . . .

Several plans were proposed, and the discussions to which they gave rise were prolonged, without coming to any determination. They hesitated a long time on the advantages of the different houses which were offered: but at last they concluded upon a plan which met with general approbation: and it was resolved to lodge the Guest of the City in the City Hall itself. It was thought, with reason, that it would be adding more dignity to the manner of receiving him; and drawing closer the ties of hospitality which were to unite the citizens of Orleans with their illustrious Guest. These considerations, offered by Mr. Roffignac, the Mayor, had the preference of all others; and the work necessary to repairing for its new appointment the immense building being occupied until then by the different offices of the Corporation, was commenced.

A rich drawing room took the place of the Council Room [*Sala Capitular*] and the magazine of arms was converted into a dining room and the offices of the Mayor, the Secretary and the Treasurer were changed into commodious chambers. The ceilings of all the rooms were embellished with cornices and rosaces [plaster rosettes]; modern chimneys [mantels] of marble replaced the clumsy ones of wood; the walls were decorated with rich and tasty hangings; and as to the furniture, everything was procured that a city, where luxury a few years since was unknown, could offer. Elegant papering and draperies, brilliant lustres [chandeliers], rich, heavy glasses [mirrors], beautiful carpets, in short nothing was spared to properly furnish what the people were already pleased to call *General Lafayette's House.*

Council records show that $15,000 was appropriated to decorate the Cabildo as a residence for the distinguished visitor. A carpet was bought for the council hall, a mirror placed over the new marble mantelpiece and a portrait of General Lafayette hung. Four dozen chairs, eight sofas, as well as tables, chandeliers and curtains were provided. The city government moved out of the Cabildo and rented a house from Baron Pontalba as a temporary City Hall.

Leaving Mobile on his tour, the Lafayette party boarded the steamboat *Natchez* on April 8, and after a stormy voyage through Mississippi Sound in which everybody became seasick, the following day steamed up the river to the Chalmette battlefield. Sunday, April 10, was a miserable, rainy day but the general was met on the levee by troops of cavalry and huge crowds, and saluted by shouts of welcome and the firing of cannon. At the Macarty plantation house, which just ten years before had been General Andrew Jackson's headquarters at the battle of New Orleans, he was met by Governor Henry Johnson who welcomed him with an appropriate speech. A little later, Lafayette, accompanied by Governor Johnson, former Governor Villeré and Lafayette's old friend and aide-de-camp in the American Revolution, Armand Duplantier, headed a procession by riding in a landau drawn by six iron gray horses. In a barouche which followed were the general's son, George Washington Lafayette and his secretary, Colonel A. Levasseur. The procession was directed by ten marshals and consisted of carriages in which rode highly placed federal, state and city officials followed by many citizens. The throng on the way was so great that the procession was a long time on the muddy road to town.

At the Place d'Armes despite the dreary weather there was a tremendous crowd to welcome the distinguished guest:

> ... the sight of a triple row of vessels that line the levee, their flags and signals flying, the thunder of the artillery on land and water, the ringing of the bells, the sound of martial music, and the continued acclamations of an immense multitude, produced a feeling that cannot be described.

Crowds such as this gathered in front of the Cabildo many times to view parades and public ceremonies.   *Ballou's Pictorial.*

73

A massive, ornate triumphal arch had been erected in the square and Mayor Roffignac welcomed Lafayette under it. After a suitable reply the general was escorted to the Presbytère (then the courthouse) where he was met by the city council and was addressed by Denis Prieur, the recorder. Lafayette then was shown to the Cabildo, "Lafayette's House". Placing himself on the balcony he reviewed the pride of Louisiana military companies who marched by in the rain. These were the Louisiana Guards, the Grenadiers, the Dragoons, the Franks, the Voltigeurs, the Union Guards, the Chasseurs, the Orleans Guards, and the Lafayette Guards, the Riflemen and a company of a hundred Choctaw Indians who came, Indian fashion, in single file. The latter, under the leadership of Captain Harper, had been encamped near New Orleans for nearly a month waiting to see "the great warrior, the brother of the great father, Washington."

The General, enfeebled by long political imprisonment in Olmütz, had to be supported as he walked. Despite his infirmities he was highly enthusiastic about his reception and to every speech made by various officials he made gracious and appropriate replies.

Then followed five days of the most hectic activities — activities which would have worn down a younger man but which Lafayette enjoyed to the utmost without apparent physical strain.

Monday, April 11:	He received visits of representatives of the legislature and members of the bar. Received guests — called on the governor and the mayor and several ladies. Went to the American Theatre (early) and the Théâtre d'Orléans (later).
Tuesday, April 12:	Received visitors from 11 to 3. Received a delegation of New Orleans Spaniards. Met a deputation of Knights Templars: received a delegation from the State Militia and from the Louisiana Legion, (whose leaders afterwards quarreled among themselves about protocol). Attended a brilliant ball in his honor at the Théâtre d'Orléans which was followed by a supper attended by hundreds of the elite of New Orleans.
Wednesday, April 13:	Received visitors, notably priests and Père Antoine, straightened out differences between the leaders of the Militia and the Legion. Made more calls on "ladies . . .

and distinguished persons". Viewed a parade and maneuvers of a battalion of artillery in the Place d'Armes in the afternoon. That evening the Place d'Armes was illuminated, hundreds of colored lamps being hung on the iron fence, in the trees and on the triumphal arch. The Cathedral, Cabildo and Presbytere were "superbly illuminated" and many citizens' houses were decorated with emblems and transparencies and a great crowd circulated through the streets. General Lafayette, in a carriage, rode twice around the square to the applause of the crowds. To climax the celebration a salvo of a hundred guns was fired and rockets were set off from the top of the arch. Lafayette then went again to the American Theatre and the Théâtre d'Orléans and finished the evening at the St. Philip Street Theatre where he attended another ball.

Thursday, April 14: Received more visitors than usual, among them delegations from the free people of color, the medical society, the marshals who had directed his entry into the city. In the evening he attended a meeting of the Grand Lodge of Louisiana with his brother masons, ate supper with 300 of them and topped off these functions by again attending the Théâtre d'Orléans to hear the Opera *Aline* and a piece written especially for the occasion, *Lafayette in New Orleans.*

Friday, April 15: The day of departure. Great crowds called to say goodbye and Lafayette left the Cabildo on foot, passed between rows of Legionaires in the Place d'Armes until he reached Levee Street where he got into a carriage which carried him to the steamboat for his journey to Baton Rouge, his next stop.

Writing in restrospect, Lafayette's secretary, Colonel Levasseur, who accompanied the general on his travels, said this about their visit to New Orleans:

I will not attempt to describe the elaborate social entertainments, which, by the beauty and amiable character of the ladies of New Orleans, the enthusiastic feeling and cordiality of the citizens, the watchful care and thoughtful profusion of their arrangements, equalled everything we had seen.

The Calaboose (1803-1914)

In the rear of the Cabildo was the calaboose or city prison. Probably the best known character ever to be incarcerated in it was one of the notorious pirate brothers, Pierre Lafitte. Charged with aiding and abetting a pair of piratical figures named Johness and Johannot who had captured two Spanish vessels, Pierre was arrested on June 6, 1814, thrown in the calaboose and indicted by the grand jury. Bail was refused since the federal authorities were determined to break up the Barataria establishment from which they operated.

Meanwhile, in Barataria on September 3, Pierre's brother Jean had met with Captain Nicholas Lockyer of the British forces who had come to Louisiana to capture New Orleans. Lockyer brought a tempting offer to the Lafittes to join their forces in the coming operation. Jean cannily put off Lockyer and sent word to Governor Claiborne through his New Orleans friend and confidant Jean Blanque, offering his services to the United States. From a letter that Jean Lafitte wrote to Blanque on September 4, 1814 it is clear that one of Lafitte's motives was to effect the release of his brother Pierre, who, suffering from illness, had been languishing in the jail for three months confined by foot and wrist irons. Before the astonished governor and his advisors could ponder over Jean's letter, Pierre mysteriously escaped from prison in the early hours of September 5. Shortly afterward the keeper of the prison inserted this advertisement in the *Louisiana Courier:*

1000 Dollars Reward.

WILL be paid for the apprehending of *PIERRE LAFITTE,* who broke and escaped last night from the prison of the parish. Said Pierre Lafitte is about 5 fet 10 inches high, stout made, light complexion and somewhat cross-eyed, further description is considered unnecessary as he is very well known in this city.

Said Lafitte took with him three negroes, to wit—Sam, formerly the property of M. Sawza, Ceasar the property of Mr. Pierre Lefebvre, and Hamilcar the property of Mr. Jarnais, the above reward will be paid to any person delivering the said Lafitte to the subscriber and fifty dollars for each of the negroes.

J. H. HOLLAND,

Sept. 7.   *Keeper of the prison.*

The advertisement offering the $1000 reward ran in the newspaper for more than a month after Pierre's jail break, but no one ever turned him in to claim the reward.

Pierre Lafitte returned to Barataria, and five days after his escape he penned a letter to Governor Claiborne approving his brother Jean's actions and seconding his offer to aid.

The so-called Lafitte cell which has been pointed out for many years as the cell in which Pierre Lafitte was confined. No substantial evidence supports the authenticity of the tale as the prisons were remodeled and rebuilt several times during the Cabildo's long and eventful history.
(photographed in 1940)   *Louisiana State Museum Collection.*

A century and a half ago it was the practice of the city authorities to send fettered negro convicts to clean the streets'. Their chains made escape difficult but did not prevent the prisoners from doing manual labor. On a couple of occasions fires broke out while the gang was working and in the excitement, some of the negroes "accidentally" escaped, chains and all. The warden of the police prison requested that he be authorized to buy a dozen new chains. This was on February 6, 1830, but the council was slow to act and six months later he was back again asking for money to buy chains as "almost fifty negroes are kept idle in the police prison due to lack of chains to send them to work."

Among the objects which may be viewed at the Cabildo is the old stocks, a pillory which was used to punish minor offenders. In the early nineteenth century stocks were mounted on a platform in the Place d'Armes and culprits, with placards inscribed with their name and offense hung about their necks, were con-

On October 23, 1827, an observor in the *Bee* wrote: "Yesterday for the first time a party of convicts condemned to hard labor went out in a costume analogous to what they have in other countries; that is to say that they were dressed in red from head to foot. We believe we perceived that they bore a considerable weight of chains."

fined in them. This picturesque type of punishment, which exposed the offender to public derision, was meted out to both whites and negroes until an act of legislature approved March 11, 1827 prohibited the sentencing of white persons to "public exposure in the pillory." The stocks, however, were used to punish negro miscreants until 1847.

As the city continued to grow, so did the population of its jail, the "Calaboose" in the rear of the City Hall. In 1813 the calaboose was a conglomeration of cells of earlier buildings, some of which dated to 1730. A grand jury inspected the place and published a report in the *Louisiana Courier* on July 2, 1813. It called attention to the near ruinious state of the "very low, humid and infectuous vaults" on the first floor which were "very unfit to lodge men whatever crimes they may be guilty". The jury viewed "with sorrow that insane persons were confined to individual cells while debtors and state's prisoners were crowded together".

The cells were still horribly overcrowded in 1823 when about fifty of the 160 persons incarcerated in it attempted a mass outbreak. Seizing a turnkey before he had had the opportunity of locking the last of three gates to the prison, they were only foiled by the efforts of a young negro guard at the outer gate. At the risk of his life, he secured the gate and threw the key into the street. Since he was on the inside with the desperate felons he quickly fled to another part of the jail and hid in a chimney. The prisoners then procured a large iron bar and proceeded to beat the lock but before they could break out the police drove them back into the prison courtyard. From the yard some of the prisoners went to the dungeon — knocked off the locks of two of the doors and ripped several planks from the floors. These they hastily carried to the gallery and attempted to make a scaffold to enable them to gain the roof of the rear prison. By this time police and citizens had surrounded the jail and when one of the prisoners ascended the roof he was shot and wounded. Other prisoners attempted to cut a hole through the floor over a room in the jailer's quarters and while they were at work a shot which came through a street window instantly killed one of them. This so stunned the convicts that they soon gave up their attempt to break out. The ringleaders were put in irons and a company of cannoneers was sent to guard the jail until things quieted down. The *Louisiana Gazette*, which reported the incident September 23, 1823, was high in its praise of Mayor Roffignac who had directed operations and of the police and volunteer firemen who had helped. The brave little negro was rescued unhurt from his chimney.

It was once possible to have one's slave whipped in the calaboose if corporal punishment had to be meted out to a disobedient or refractory slave. An ordinance passed by the city council on September 25, 1830 authorized the warden to charge 25¢ for every slave whipped in the police prison, the 25¢ to be paid by the person bringing the slave to be whipped.

An interesting glimpse, from a policeman's point of view, of night-life occurrences in New Orleans a century and half ago has survived in the form of a report by Edouard Cardinaud, captain of the police guard at City Hall. Dated January 18, 1818, it reads:

"At 8 o'clock in the evening, Sieur Joseph Gamache brought to the station a negro named Honoré, a run-away since two weeks, saying that he belonged to Mr. Mccarty, planter, upriver, having at the end of his handkerchief six dollars. The said handkerchief and money deposited at the station. The Sieur Gamache will present himself at the office of the mayor. Honoré put in jail.

At 10 o'clock in the evening, the faubourg Marigny patrol arrested a negro named Célestin belonging to Sieur Chapron, taken in said faubourg. The negro having made resistance to the guard, he was put in jail.

At 10:30 o'clock the south patrol brought to the station individuals taken in drink, found sleeping on the banquette of Royal and St. Peter streets. They have been put in the disciplinary cell.

The concert at Sieur Davis's took place [Théâtre d'Orléans]. The ball at Sieur Tremoulet's took place [Tremoulet's Hotel]. The ball of St. Martin took place [Salle Condé]. That of the Union took place [a quadroon ballroom on Ursulines Street]."

Except for the runaway slaves, how like today with drunks on Royal Street and three balls and a concert in the same evening!

Joseph Holt Ingraham, in his *Southwest by a Yankee,* published in 1835, showed a greater interest in the old prison in the rear than he did in the Cabildo itself; he wrote:

> . . . we passed the famous Calaboos, or Calabozo, the city prison, so celebrated by all seamen who have made the voyage to New Orleans, and who in their "long yarns" upon the forecastle, in their weary watches, fail not to clothe it with every horror of which the Calcutta black hole, or the Dartmoor prison — two horrible bugbears to sailors — could boast. Its external appearance, however, did not strike me as very appalling. It is a long plain, plastered, blackened building, with grated windows, looking gloomy enough but not more so than a common country jail. It is built close upon the street, and had not my companion observed as we passed along, "That is the Calaboos," I should not probably have remarked it. On the corner above, and fronting the "square" is the guardhouse, or quarters of the gens d' armes. Several of them in their plain blue uniforms and side arms, were lounging about the corner as we passed, mingling and conversing with persons in citizens' dress. A glance *en passant* through an open door, disclosed an apparently well filled armory."

By the early 1830's the city council, realizing that something had to be done about its prison, had the city engineer Joseph Pilié make plans to enlarge it. At that time the prison extended back of the Cabildo on sites now occupied by the Arsenal, the Jackson House, the Maison Créole, Cabildo Alley, and four of the Labranche Buildings (now numbers 823-25 St. Peter Street) and two buildings in their rear. Pilié planned a large addition in 1833, but the city council changed its mind and decided to build a still larger prison on Orleans and St. Ann streets (in the rear of the present municipal auditorium). By the time the Orleans Street (Parish) prison was completed in 1837, a report of the grand jury of that year commented on the soon-to-be vacated calaboose:

> "The old Calaboose is a horrible residence for any human being, no matter what his guilt may be . . . Innocent men accused of no criminal offense and seamen suspected of a design to desert their vessel are mingled with convicts and the very dregs of the human race in a space much too limited . . ."

Shortly afterwards, the rear portion of the old calaboose was demolished, the site immediately adjacent to the Cabildo deeded to the state for the construction of the Arsenal building, and the rest of the site sold to private owners.

An interesting sidelight on the old prison was the attempt in 1831 of some prisoners to escape by tunneling under the prison wall next to the street. After considerable burrowing they found themselves in a subterranean vault "from which escape seemed impossible." They were discovered and returned to their cells and the affair forgotten until 1840, when the Labranche Buildings were being erected, the "subterranean cell" was uncovered by workmen digging the foundations. This discovery produced a sensation and all the newspapers of February 18th printed the story. The *Daily Picayune* carried the headline:

"An Underground Affair"

and reported that

> "Yesterday while the workmen were excavating for building lots lately sold by the First Municipality on the square formerly occupied by the old prisons, between St. Peter and Orleans streets, vaults were discovered at the depth of eight feet below the surface of the earth, arched with strong iron bars, on which thick brick foundations had been formerly built. In one of the vaults we learn there was found a gold crucifix weighing 28 pounds, and also a quantity of human bones. At the bottom of this vault a door was discovered apparently leading to vaults still deeper."

The discovery attracted throngs of the curious and speculation was rampant on the probable use of these mysterious vaults. They were variously declared to be secret Jesuit hiding places, dungeons of the Spanish Inquisition, or the torture chamber of a cruel Spanish governor.

The story continued to attract attention for several days; some proposed bringing an expert antiquarian from New York, others demanding that the vaults be thoroughly explored by the city. Eventually the gold crucifix was found to be only a rusty iron fire dog, and the *Bee*, less sensational than the other papers, reported that

> "An antiquarian in whose opinion we place great confidence, because he is somewhat tinctured with suspicion, assures us that it was nothing more or less than a small cellar; if not a place not to be mentioned to the refined."

Actually the "subterranean vaults" were just the cesspools of the old prison, for plans and a description of a large and substantial two-storied privy for the prisoners still exist. Why this didn't occur to most onlookers is a mystery—every New Orleans household had a privy and such a vault on a smaller scale in its own back yard!

The same year that the "subterranean vault" was discovered (1840) the council of the first municipality adopted an ordinance' to reorganize the poorly run police department. The force, fifty-eight officers and men, was to be divided into a day and a night watch. The men were to be stationed at three posts: at City Hall, at the Faubourg Tremé and at Bayou St. John. The ground floor of the Cabildo was used as a central police station. Quartered

there were a captain, a lieutenant, a sergeant, two corporals and thirty-four constables.

Two of the men were to attend the fire bell and there was to be a sentinel at City Hall and one at the meat market. Eight lamplighters were also employed under the supervision of the captain and they were expected to aid police when called upon to do so. Their pay was $35 a month.

The constables carried no firearms; their only weapon being a spontoon or half-pike which during the night they were to strike on the pavement when they came to a corner on their beats. In case of trouble they were provided with rattles and would "spring their rattles" to call for assistance. The ordinance[1] did not specify the style of uniforms but each man on duty was required to wear "a painted leather cap, numbered to correspond with the Roll of the District in which he may serve." For his services he was paid $35 a month; corporals received $50, sergeants $60, lieutenants $100 and captains $150!

The police would pick up runaway slaves and bring them to the calaboose. Generally their owners would show up to claim them but inevitably there would be some whose owners were unknown. Public notice was given of such unclaimed slaves and those not called for were sold at public auction. One such auction, held August 30, 1845, at the City Exchange netted $2,360 which was turned over to the treasurer of the police department.

[1] The joker in the ordinance of July 27, 1840 was that the mayor and recorder "shall have the appointments of the officers and men" (except the captain and lieutenants) and all vacancies "shall be supplied by the mayor." For nearly half a century this arrangement was to bedevil the police department, for a man, even for a $35 a month job, could only expect to hold it as long as the mayor who appointed him was in office. Inefficiently organized, subject to little or no discipline, the police force was the focal point of graft and corruption during these years. It was not until a system of honorary police commissioners was inaugurated in 1888 that some progress was made in forming a stable and efficient police department.

When the rear portion of the calaboose was demolished, certain cells adjoining the Cabildo remained and were used as a police jail. In 1850, Louis Pilié designed a block of six new cells three stories in height; and these were erected and are still part of the present structure.

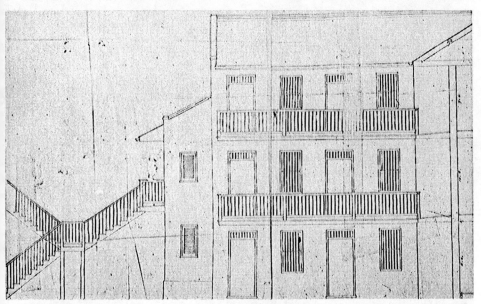

Elevation drawing of the six cells in the courtyard of the Cabildo which were built in 1850.   *Louis Pilié, Architect.*

In 1910 a newspaper writer described the police jail at the Cabildo which was then called the Third Precinct Station:

"Everyone knows that it [the Cabildo] is built around a kind of court with stairs leaping lightly from gallery to gallery; and that these galleries are filled with cells with grated doors. The head of this station, Capt. Rawlings will tell you that the "drunks" are generally taken to the first floor cells because it is sometimes very hard to get them up the stairs on account of the general helplessness of their condition . . .
In the cells on the second floor are deposited those who can still walk. The women's cell is there; rather a large room with a bench running around the walls [and] there is a Japanese simplicity about this style of furnishing that appeals to an aesthetic soul . . .
There are cells on the third floor also, but they are otherwise engaged. Some of them are given over to a crowd of old women who go about the streets begging, basket on arm. They have no homes; then come in there at night to sleep . . ."

In 1968-69 the exterior of these cells was restored as faithfully as possible in accordance with the original drawings, although some of the upper ones now house restrooms and air-conditioning equipment, etc., instead of prisoners.

IN THE CALABOOSE.

This view of the calaboose or police jail in the courtyard of the Cabildo was sketched by Joseph Pennell in 1888.

Dr. Antommarchi's Mask (1834)

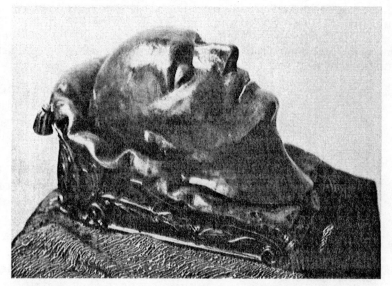

The death mask of the Emperor Napoleon Bonaparte presented to the City Council by Dr. Francisco Antommarchi.

One of the most fascinating objects in the collection of the Louisiana State Museum is the death mask of Emperor Napoleon Bonaparte This was made by Dr. Francisco Antommarchi who had attended the emperor in St. Helena when he died, and who had made a death mask of the Little Corporal.[1] Some years later in Paris he had had four bronze casts made from the mold. Coming to New Orleans in 1834, he was given a rousing welcome by the French and Creole admirers of Napoleon who still cherished memories of the great leader and the tradition of the empire. Deeply moved, he wrote to Mayor Prieur on November 12 and offered to present one of the casts to the city.

"The communication was submitted to the City Council, and it was resolved that the *souvenir* should be accepted and placed in the Council Chamber," wrote Henry C. Castellanos in his charming little book *New Orleans As It Was.*

Continuing, he penned: "No sooner had this action became known, than the French residents determined to make it the occasion of a public jubilee. The Legion was called out on the "Place d'Armes", with flags flying and drums beating. French societies, in holiday attire, and thousands of the "unattached," preceded by numerous bands playing *Partant Pour la Syrie* and the *"Marseillaise",* paraded Chartres, Royal and Bourbon streets, with

[1] The French historian Octave Aubrey states in *The Last Days of Napoleon* that the death mask was made by the English physician, Dr. Francis Burton, with Antommarchi's help; that after the plaster mold was made it was surreptitiously taken by Antommarchi who eventually had the bronze casts made without giving Burton credit or even a copy. Aubry also states that despite Antommarchi's claim of friendship with the emperor, Napoleon, during his last days despised him, and on one occasion actually ordered him out of his sight.

Dr. Antommarchi at their head, until they finally halted in front of the old "Cabildo" . . . where the presentation took place in due form. I shall not go into the details of the affair, but the reader may picture to himself, as his fancy may lead, the speeches, the wine bibbing and the toasts that usually prevailed at such public convivialities."

Dr. Francisco Antommarchi.

Antommarchi set up a medical practice in New Orleans but left in 1838 for Mexico. He died at sea while on a trip to Cuba.

Subsequently, the death mask has had a very curious history. It remained in the council chamber of the Cabildo for some years. When the new City Hall (now Gallier Hall) was completed in 1853, the mask was removed to the new building where it was displayed in the council chamber. After the Civil War, in 1866, the City Hall was remodeled and in some manner the mask was thrown out on a pile of trash. By the merest chance it caught the eye of Adam Giffen, a highly respected gentleman, formerly the city treasurer. Before it could be carted away by the junk dealer who had bought the discarded materials, Giffen then and there bought the mask and kept it in the parlor of his home until he died in the 1890's. It was then given to the widow of Robert Giffen, Adam's son, who also kept it in her home. In 1896 Captain William G. Raoul, a native Louisianian who had been president of the Central of Georgia Railway, bought the cast for $500 "for personal reasons" and took it to his home in Atlanta where it was placed in storage. Curiosity as to what happened to the cast, now gone from public view for more than 40 years, caused Mrs. Olivia Blanchard to start a search for its whereabouts. With the help of publicity by the *New Orleans Item* the mask was rediscovered and Captain Raoul thereupon offered to return it to the city. In February, 1909, his offer was gratefully accepted by Mayor Martin Behrman and the mask returned to New Orleans where it was placed in the custody of the Louisiana State Museum.

In 1932, a jobless salesman attempted to steal the mask but E. L. Carrol, a medical student at Tulane University, then serving as a night watchman at the Cabildo, caught the thief and the mask was again saved.

Troubled Times — The Cabildo under Gunfire
(1858, 1873, 1874, 1877)

Headquarters of the New Orleans Vigilance Committee.
From Ballou's Pictorial Drawing Room Companion,
July 10, 1858.

Four times in its history the Cabildo was the object of attack by armed men. The first of these affairs took place in June 1858, just before the municipal election in which Gerard Stith ran against Major P. G. T. Beauregard for mayor. A large group of citizens, aroused over the disorders which were the usual accompaniment of elections in New Orleans, secretly organized a vigilance committee and without fanfare took possession of Jackson Square, occupied the court rooms of the Cabildo, seized the arsenal in its rear and armed themselves with the weapons in it. This group under Captain Johnson K. Duncan then publicly announced its intention of taking over the civil government of the city to insure a fair election without the "disorder, outrage and unchecked assassination" which usually accompanied election campaigns in New Orleans. The affair occurred during the time that the American or "Know-Nothing" party was active, and there were of course other political overtones.

For five days the Vigilance Committee, Mayor Waterman, candidate Stith, the City Council, and an opposition group numbering 1,600 hastily sworn in as police deputies conferred, pleaded, threatened, and did everything but fight. Then came election day, "one of the most orderly in the history of the city", in which

The McEnery militia and the Metropolitan police fight for the possession of the 3rd precinct police station in the Cabildo.

From Frank Leslie's Illustrated Newspaper, March 22, 1873.

the American party of Stith won and the Vigilance Committee evacuated its position and faded away. Unfortunately, five members of Duncan's men were accidentally killed during the occupation of Fort Vigilance, as the Cabildo was dubbed, and when the occupying force abandoned the "fort" they left behind a monumental pile of rubbish which had to be cleaned up before the courts could again function.

A second violent episode occurred in 1873 during Reconstruction times. This was the period in which Louisiana was struggling to rid the state of carpetbag rule. There were two governors and two legislatures, and the carpetbag regime of Governor Kellogg was sustained by the Metropolitan Police, which was composed largely of negroes, and by federal troops stationed in the city. Increasing friction between the negroes and whites, and the arrogance and abusiveness of the negroes who were predominant in city and state councils led to a mass meeting of citizens who determined to make an effort to rid the city of the corruption which was strangling it. The Metropolitan Police was a symbol of the hated Kellogg regime and the citizens determined to dislodge them from the third precinct police station in the Cabildo.

About 9:30 p.m. on the night of March 5, 1873, sixty-five members of the McEnery state militia led by General Frederick N. Ogden marched to Jackson Square and opened fire on the Cabildo. The police returned the fire and General Ogden was slightly wounded, but the militia, now reinforced and some 300 strong, re-formed in the shelter of the Cathedral. The Metropolitans then came out of the Cabildo to fight. They had superior numbers and a cannon which they had some trouble in unlimbering, and for about fifteen minutes there was continuous musketry firing. While the fighting was under way, a detachment of United States troops arrived and their commander ordered the militia to disperse, which they did. One man was killed and seven wounded in the melee.

Next year the Metropolitans were still in the Cabildo. On September 14, several hundred of them (two battalions of infantry, a battery, and an escort of cavalry) marched to Canal Street near the river to give battle to the Crescent City White League, an aroused citizen-army, again trying to rid the state of the hated Kellogg government. One of their leaders, General A. S. Badger, fell seriously wounded in the fierce fight which ensued and the Metropolitans wavered, broke and fled to the shelter of the Customhouse and back to the Cabildo, leaving eleven men killed on the ground. Next day the badly demoralized negro militia in the State House surrendered, as did the Metropolitans in the Cabildo and in the arsenal in its rear. But victory was to be short-lived. Governor McEnery's government was soon forced out by the arrival of United States troops sent by President Grant, and Kellogg's Metropolitans were again in the Cabildo to stay for three more long years.

New Orleans had been under dictatorial rule for fifteen years when in 1877 an election was held which again produced two governors and two legislatures. A show of force and determination by the local citizenry culminated in the withdrawal of the military regime and the return of home rule in Louisiana. On January 8, 1877, Francis T. Nicholls was elected governor of Louisiana and inaugurated with great public ceremony at St. Patrick's Hall on Camp Street (opposite Lafayette Square) which also housed this faction's legislature. The rival government of S. N. Packard barricaded itself in the State House (the old St. Louis Hotel) where Packard was inaugurated behind closed doors. The situation was again very tense, and on the morning of January 9, about 3,000 citizens and members of the Crescent City White League with rifles and field pieces met at Lafayette Square, again with General Frederick N. Ogden at their head, and marched to Jackson Square. Their object was to drive out

The Dual State Government in Louisiana — Seizure of the Supreme Court Building at New Orleans by the State Militia under command of General Ogden, January 19, 1877.

From Frank Leslie's Illustrated Newspaper, January 27, 1877.

the Metropolitans occupying the police station in the Cabildo and to secure the Supreme Court chamber on its second floor, in which, as late as that morning, the Supreme Court officials of Packard's faction had still been functioning. The White League and its cohorts had instructions to seat the previously appointed justices of the Nicholls administration in the Supreme Court chamber and thus complete the executive, legislative and judicial branches of the state government. The exciting events which followed were vividly penned by John Smith Kendall in his *History of New Orleans*. Kendall used an eye-witness account of the affair told him by J. D. Hill:

> Among the officers on duty this day was J. D. Hill, a member of the House, who had obtained leave of absence in order to participate in the operations. As the troops approached the Cabildo he sent Lieut. Oscar Nixon, one of Ogden's aides-de-camp, to ask permission from the commanding officer to take Capt. Archie Mitchell's company and seize the building. This was granted. Mitchell's company fell out of the column, and, led by Hill, turned to the left into St. Ann Street. [St. Peter Street?] Hill halted the command under the arches of the Cabildo, with the right deployed towards the Cathedral. He then went to the door of the police station and demanded of Captain Lawler, in command there, that he surrender the building. Lawler refused. Half of Lawler's men were collected in the police station, the remainder occupied a position half way up the staircase leading to the upper floor and the Supreme Court room. A demand made upon the latter to open the gates and admit the citizen soldiery was likewise refused. While Lawler was kept busy with pretended negotiations by one of the other officers of the militia, Hill and his men burst the chain which secured the iron gate opening on the main stair and effected an entrance. In the meantime the Nicholls court had assembled in a room on St. Ann Street. As soon as the gate swung open the Metropolitans retreated up the stairs into the courtroom, without attempting any resistance. Hill sent for the judges, taking Judge Alcibiade de Blanc on his arm, escorted him to the upper floor, followed by Lieutenant Gibson with the chief justice, T. C. Manning. The cowed Metropolitans were compelled to assemble in a corner of the room, with their hats respectfully removed and their arms piled against the wall, while Hill, having seen his charges seated on the bench, assumed the role of cryer, and formally proclaimed the court ready for business . . .
>
> Hill then descended to the gateway, where his men were in waiting. Captain Lawler, informed that this mission entrusted to him had failed, consented to surrender. His men were informed that they might return to their homes. Many were afraid to do so, apprehending mistreatment at the hands of the populace, to whom the sight of their uniform was as a red cloak to a bull. Mitchell accordingly detailed some of his command to accompany them, and they were in this manner enabled to get safely to their residences.

The Radical legislators, however, stayed holed up in the State House (St. Louis Hotel) for nearly four months until a commission sent from Washington, realizing that unwarrantable wrong was being perpetuated, sought to bring about the establishment of the Nicholls government. This and certain defections from the Packard partisans and other factors caused the eventual disintegration of the carpetbag regime and on April 24, 1877 the last of the federal troops left New Orleans, this time for good, and the Packard regime collapsed.

A badge worn by the Metropolitan Police.
Courtesy Major Henry M. Morris,
Chief of Detectives,
New Orleans Police Department.

In 1900 bluestocking Mme. A. G. Durno offered the opinion that the century old Cabildo which at that time housed the Supreme Court, the Second Recorder's Court, the Third Precinct Police Station and jail was not well adapted for these purposes. Writing in *Rightor's Standard History of New Orleans, Louisiana* she states:

> Some iconoclastic individuals have suggested tearing it down, but the proposal brought out a storm of protest from citizens who are interested in the preservation of the few remaining monuments of the past, and it is not probable that it will ever be carried out.

The Louisiana Historical Society, Mme. Durno wrote, was thinking of repairing and preserving the Cabildo and turning it into a historical museum in time to celebrate the Centenary of the Louisiana Purchase in 1903.

This idea brought fruit twelve years later when the Louisiana State Museum opened its doors on April 30, 1912.

The Centennial Celebration of the Louisiana Transfer and the Beginnings of the State Museum (1903, 1904, 1906, 1911)

Officials reviewing cavalry troop passing the Cabildo. This was part of the Centennial celebration of the Louisiana Purchase. (December, 1903).   *Louisiana State Museum.*

The Centennial of the Louisiana Purchase was celebrated with great pomp in New Orleans on December 18, 19 and 20, 1903. There was a gala concert at the French Opera House followed by a ball, a performance of *Carmen* at the same theatre, a high mass and *Te Deum* at the St. Louis Cathedral, a review of troops at the Cabildo and a reenactment of the transfer ceremoney in the *sala capitular*. The affair was graced by the presence of M. Jusserand, the French Ambassador to the United States, the Hon. Tuero y O'Donnel, representing Spain, Admiral W. C. Wise representing the United States, former Governor D. R. Francis of Missouri, President of the Louisiana Purchase Exposition, Governor W. W. Heard of Louisiana, Mayor Paul Capdevielle, Alcée Fortier, President of the Louisiana Historical Society and many others prominent in New Orleans.

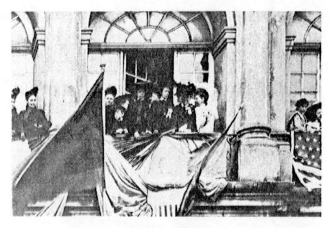

*Favored spectators view the centennial celebration from
the balcony of the Cabildo (1903).*

A replica of the Cabildo was built in 1904 in St. Louis for the
Louisiana Purchase Exposition held to commemorate the centennial of the purchase of the Louisiana Territory from France.
It was built to the exact size of the original (95 x 107 feet) and
cost $25,000. A reproduction of the equestrian statue of General
Andrew Jackson stood in the park in front of the building, and
the interior was furnished with antique furniture and ornamented
with portraits of La Salle, Livingston, Monroe, Marbois, Jefferson, Napoleon, Salcedo, Laussat, Wilkinson and Claiborne, and
a large painting of New Orleans as it was in 1803 (was this the
De Woiserie now in the Chicago Historical Society's collection?).
An antique desk, believed to have been the one on which the
transfer was signed a hundred years before, was also displayed.

*The replica of the old Cabildo constructed in St. Louis
in 1904 for the Louisiana Purchase Exposition.*

On "Louisiana Day"—September 14, 1904—Louisiana's governor, Newton C. Blanchard, came "accompanied by a staff of eighty, the historic Washington Artillery and many prominent Louisianians" and in the *sala capitular* of the mock Cabildo, a repetition of the transfer ceremonies took place. The French Colonial Prefect Laussat was represented by Prof. Alcée Fortier; Governor William C. C. Claiborne by his descendant Hon. Charles F. Claiborne; General James Wilkinson by his descendant Theodore S. Wilkinson; Daugerot, the French secretary by Lucian Soniat-Dufossat, and the American secretary M. Wadsworth by the Honorable James S. Zacherie. The American flag was raised by Pierre Chouteau, Jr., aged 6, a descendant of the founder of St. Louis, the Washington Artillery fired a salute and there was music by the eighty-six-piece band of the famous Garde Républicaine which had come to the exposition from Paris. All this was "followed by luncheons and receptions, ending in the evening . . . with eleven grand pieces of Pain's fireworks, five historic Louisiana characters and scenes including a colossal picture of the transfer after Thulstrup's great painting."

The Louisiana State Museum had its genesis in the collection of the exhibit which was sent to St. Louis to be shown in the replica of the Cabildo. The legislature had previously (in 1900) created a board of administrators and given official recognition to a projected historical museum, but had appropriated no funds to start the project. At the conclusion of the St. Louis Exposition, the board of curators of a yet-to-be-founded museum requested that the Louisiana exhibit be returned to New Orleans. After some discussion with officials of Louisiana State University, which also wanted the exhibition, New Orleans was selected as the site and the lower floor of the Washington Artillery Hall on Carondelet Street was rented. Robert Glenk as curator installed the display which was opened May 3, 1905. In 1906 the legislature passed another act creating the State Museum and provided for its permanent location and maintenance. The first board of curators of the new museum consisted of Prof. Alcée Fortier, W. O. Hart, Gen. W. D. Gardiner, Thomas P. Thompson, Prof. R. S. Cocks, Frank M. Miller, Gen. John B. Levert, J. W. Frankenbush and Henri L. Gueydan. The board met on December 10, 1906, and T. P. Thompson was elected president, and Prof. Alcée Fortier vice president, Dr. W. C. Stubbs was made general manager and treasurer, and Robert Glenk curator and secretary. The first appropriation was $5,000 and the museum grew so rapidly that the allocated space in the Washington Hall was soon overflowing.

The courtroom of the Supreme Court of Louisiana as it appeared in 1901. Part of this room had been the "Sala Capitular" in which the transfer of the Louisiana Territory had taken place in 1803, but in one of many remodelings which took place, the partitions separating it from adjacent rooms had been removed to form a much larger space. The justices sat on a dais before a rich crimson damask hanging and the bar was ornamented with the busts of Judges Martin and Marshall and jurists Edward Livingston and Pierre Soulé. One of the walls was covered with the portraits of distinguished members of bench and bar, among them Hennen, Roselius, Grymes, Slidell, and Judge Rost. Spectators sat in cane-bottomed chairs. The room was heated by a cast-iron stove and cooled by electric ceiling fans suspended from a pressed steel ceiling. In the restoration work which took place in 1968-69, the partition was replaced to give the room the same character it had when the transfer took place in 1803.

In the 1890's when the Supreme Court (then housed on the second floor of the Cabildo) was in session, traffic in the surrounding streets was suspended because of the noise created by wagon wheels passing over the Belgian blocks with which the streets were paved. To insure quiet, chains were stretched across St. Ann, St. Peter and Chartres Streets to stop all wheeled traffic.

Courthouse, Jackson Square — putting up the chain barrier when court is in session. Water color sketch by W. A. Rogers, from Harper's Weekly, December 30, 1899.

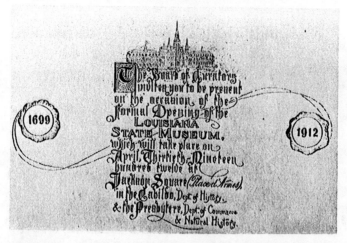

Invitation to the formal opening of the Louisiana State Museum, April 30, 1912.

About this time the new (now old) Court House on Royal and St. Louis streets was being constructed and on June 30, 1908 the city council of New Orleans passed an ordinance which placed the Cabildo, then used as a courthouse and police station, and the Presbytère under the supervision of the board of curators of the Louisiana State Museum. The Louisiana Historical Society was given the use of the soon-to-be-vacated chamber of the supreme court *(sala capitular)*. After the court moved to its new quarters in the .fall of 1910, tho board remodeled the building for use as a museum and it was opened to visitors on April 17, 1911 "with a very creditable exhibit of historical matters and oil paintings lent and donated by public spirited citizens." So great was the amount of material accumulated that 200 wagon loads of artifacts, paintings and natural history objects, in all 20,000 items, were moved to the new museum.

The police station and the Second City Criminal Court which occupied the lower floor of the Cabildo were not turned over to the Louisiana State Museum until 1914.

Thousands of objects, documents, books, pictures, furniture, war relics, costumes, natural history specimens, came in a steady flow to the Louisiana State Museum and filled the Cabildo and its sister-building, the Presbytère. Reports of the board of curators in the 1920's reflect the steady increase of accessions by gift, loan and occasional purchase. The museum was handicapped by low state appropriations, but the hard work of its curator Robert Glenk and his staff, under the wise directions of the board of curators, made up for lack of funds. Glenk and his staff made display cases, restored oil paintings, did taxidermy and kept the museum open every day of the year except Christmas Day!

The Cabildo as the Louisiana State Museum

ROBERT GLENK,

Robert Glenk (1870-1950).
The "Father" of the
Louisiana State Museum.

The Louisiana State Museum became a cultural center and during 1920-21 no less than fifty lectures on historical, chemical, engineering and entomological subjects were delivered there. The Louisiana Historical Society, founded in 1836, has had permanent use of the *sala capitular* since 1915 and in this era the Louisiana Engineering Society, the Louisiana section of the American Association of Engineers, and the Louisiana Entomological Society held their meetings there.

Robert Glenk, B.S., Ph.C., was selected "Secretary and Custodian" of the newly formed Louisiana State Museum in 1906. For the next twenty-eight years this "father of the Louisiana State Museum" was its curator. From 1914 until the end of his career at the Museum he was aided by "honorary curators," specialists in various fields, among whom were Edward Foster (Invertebrates, also coins and medals); L. S. Frierson (Mollusks); Harry Kopman and Stanley Clisby Arthur (Birds); George Williamson (Archeology); M. L. Alexander (Birds and Mammals); Charles H. Behre, Jr. (Paleontology); Henry P. Dart (Archives of Louisiana); Percy P. Viosca, Jr. (Fishes and Reptiles); Dr. Isaac M. Cline (Paintings); Dr. Ellsworth Woodward and R. B. Foster (Art); and Professor Henry Wehrmann, (Music).

In 1934 James J. A. Fortier became executive director, serving until 1940. He was succeeded in December 1940 by André Chanet who served until June 1941 when Stanley Clisby Arthur became executive director. Arthur served until 1948 when he was succeeded by S. P. Revere (1948-1952), Benjamin B. Matthews (1953-1954), Lester B. Bridaham (1954-1956), Charles E. Frampton (Business Manager 1956-1964) and Mrs. Peggy E. Richards, Director, from 1964 to 1973.

"I have the great honor in standing on this historic ground to receive the greetings of my countrymen, and to recall the fact that here, nearly a hundred years ago, the great transaction took place that dedicated a larger area than the original thirteen states to liberty and union forever."
— President William McKinley
at the Cabildo May 2, 1901.
With him are Governor W. W. Heard
and Mayor Paul Capdevielle.

William McKinley was the first president of the United States to visit New Orleans while in office. He had come on May 1, 1901, accompanied by his wife, and that evening the citizens gave him a banquet. The next day he visited the Cabildo where he was met by a delegation of notable Louisianians, including the governor, the mayor, and justices of the Supreme Court. Alcée Fortier, president of the Louisiana Historical Society, sketched the history of Louisiana for the assembled guests and the president was presented to a large gathering in the streets below from the balcony of the Cabildo.

New Orleans, with the rest of the nation, was saddened when just four months later the news came of the president's assassination.

* * *

The Cabildo suffered severe damage in the hurricane which struck New Orleans on September 29, 1915. The wind, accompanied by a furious rain, blew continuously for twenty-four hours with a velocity that reached 120 miles an hour, and the barometer reached a low of 28.11 inches. The old building stood the storm very well until the wind reached a velocity of over 100 miles an hour, when one after another the window panes were blown in, and finally some of the window and door frames gave way. Slates and chimneys were blown away and the courtyard was piled high with a mass of slates, bricks and timbers from the roofs of neighboring buildings, and particularly from the adjoining Cathedral. The interior was a shambles with wrecked show cases, door frames and broken glass. One piece of slate went through a window and struck a portrait of Mrs. Jefferson Davis and remained affixed there.

Luckily the curators of the museum were able to obtain roofing paper and in two days the staff had the roof of the building fairly tight. This was fortunate, for in the two weeks which followed the storm, twenty-six inches of rain fell, and in many cases caused more damage than the hurricane.

The Presbytère, then occupied by the Museum of Natural History, was also severely damaged and new roofs, many windows and doors, and 560 window lights had to be replaced in the two buildings.

This reenactment of the Louisiana Purchase transfer took place in the "Sala Capitular" on December 20, 1926. Among those present were James Wilkinson, a descendant of General James Wilkinson (second from the left) and Duralde Claiborne, a descendant of Governor William C. C. Claiborne (with mustache). Other participants were Charles J. Rivet, H. M. Gill, André Lafargue, Walter S. Lewis, W. J. Warrington, H. L. Gueydan, Arthur McGuirk, Clarence J. Cocks, and George C. H. Kernion.
Louisiana State Museum collection.

Depression Days (the 1930's)

The Great Depression was late in striking New Orleans, but when it did, thousands of its people were out of work, the Works Progress Administration was inaugurated by the federal government, and the Louisiana State Museum reaped a permanent benefit. In 1935 a record preservation project was started employing 105 persons, and the immense amounts of data, documents, newspapers, letters, books, files, and objects, which for lack of personnel and appropriations had not been filed, indexed, catalogued, labeled, copied, translated or repaired, were put in some semblance of order. In the two years 1936-1937, more than 60,000 pages of documents were translated, thousands of books, magazines and pamphlets were checked, catalogued and shelved, nearly 2,000,000 index cards typed, some 42,000 pictures classified and filed, and a survey made of inscriptions on tombs and

monuments in New Orleans cemeteries. The unemployed architects of the city were put to work and under the Historic American Buildings Survey they measured many of the historic buildings of the Vieux Carré. Complete measured drawings of the
Cabildo were made, one of which appears in this book. In addition, the Works Progress Administration by July 1937, had spent
$35,500 repairing the Cabildo plus $15,200 for installing a sprinkler
system, $9,000 for repairing the Arsenal and $13,000 for rebuilding Jackson House, the former home of James Dowlin.

The Arsenal.

*Photograph by
Richard Koch.*

The Arsenal, Jackson House and the Calabozo (1839-1842)

Directly in back of the Cabildo is the Arsenal. Constructed
as a state armory from plans of the architect-builders Dakin
and Dakin in 1839, this building, with its striking Greek-revival
design, is an interesting landmark. From 1846 until the Civil War
it was used by the Orleans Artillery. In 1858 it was seized by the
Vigilance Committee; in 1860 it was used as headquarters for
General P. G. T. Beauregard, adjutant general of Louisiana. In

the early days of the Civil War the Confederates used it to store military supplies, and after the occupation of New Orleans by the Federals it became a military prison. During Reconstruction times the Metropolitan Police used it and it was to its sheltering walls they fled after their hasty retreat in the battle of September 14, 1874 on the riverfront. In later years it was used by the reorganized Orleans Artillery and as a state arsenal. On March 15, 1914, it was transferred to the Louisiana State Museum. After restorative work, this building was opened on January 9, 1915 as a feature of the centennial celebration of the Battle of New Orleans, and used for the display of relics of the military engagements in which Louisiana had participated.

In 1921 William Ratcliffe Irby, the philantropist who had done so much for the preservation movement in New Orleans, acquired the lower Pontalba building from its absentee owners in France, and the Dowlin house on St. Peter Street next to the Arsenal. The Pontalba building was bequeathed to the Louisiana State Museum at Mr. Irby's death in 1926, and the Dowlin house which was in poor structural state was demolished and reconstructed as a Works Progress Administration project sponsored by the museum in 1936. The lower floor is the home of the Chalmette Chapter, National Society United States Daughters of 1812, who call it Jackson House. The Colonial Dames Resident in Louisiana formerly had headquarters on the second floor.

The old house known for years as the Calabozo since it was built on the site of the old prison was also given to the museum by Mr. Irby (1922). This building, which also dates from 1842, was dedicated by representatives of the French government as La Maison Créole (the Creole House) at ceremonies commemorating the 250th anniversary of the death of the French explorer La Salle, and a medal commemorating the event was struck in honor of the occasion.

The Louisiana Colonials once had their headquarters in this building but it is at present unused.

General Chairman E. V. Richards opens the Sesquicentennial Celebration of the Louisiana Purchase from a gallery in the courtyard of the Cabildo, April 30, 1953.
Louisiana State Museum.

The Sesquicentennial Celebration of the Louisiana Transfer (1953)

In 1953 the Cabildo was the center of cultural interest in connection with the sesquicentennial celebration of the Louisiana Purchase. An exhibition of pictures, books and documents in-including a rare copy of the Purchase document itself was gathered by the museum in co-operation with the Louisiana Landmarks Society and the exhibition was officially opened in the courtyard of the Cabildo in April. Later that year the French government sent many interesting items and another exhibition called *France-Louisiana* was officially opened by the French ambassador to the United States, Henri Bonnet, on October 16.

The celebration was climaxed by a visit to New Orleans by President Dwight D. Eisenhower on October 17. A viewing stand had been constructed at Jackson Square for the President, state and city officials and other dignitaries. In costume, three descendants of Laussat, Claiborne and Wilkinson, the original signers of the *procés verbal*, (Anthony Laussat Geyelin of Villanova, Pa., Dr. Duralde Claiborne and James Wilkinson III) reenacted the drama of December 20, 1803, signing a replica of the document in the Square. They then ascended the stand and introduced themselves to the President who shook their hands. President Eisenhower then signed the replica himself as did Governor Robert F. Kennon and Mayor de Lesseps S. Morrison.

The President then viewed a typical carnival parade and the *Times-Picayune* next day commented, "This was the first time Rex and Comus marched out of season and they shared a common throne on the lead float, Comus on the right waving his cup and Rex on the left with his scepter."

Display of the Louisiana Historical Society.
    (Probably about 1909).

View of the cluttered gallery of the Cabildo in 1937. Louisiana State Museum.

Part of Louisiana Purchase Sesquicentennial Exhibition
Cabildo   1953

In 1953 the gallery was cleared and the Sesquicentennial Exhibition set up.

The Restoration of the Cabildo (1966-1969)

As has been pointed out in the preceding account, the Cabildo has undergone a continuing series of renovations and remodelings ever since it was first completed a hundred and seventy years ago. It has, however, through all these vicissitudes, preserved the basic character given to it by its architect Guillemard when he incorporated the ruins of the old corps de garde into his essentially new design.

No major renovations of the Cabildo had been undertaken by the Louisiana State Museum since the extensive work that was accomplished by the Works Progress Administration in the 1930's. The building was, by the 1960's, showing signs of deterioration and an appeal was made to the State Legislature for funds for its restoration. In 1960 a sum of $900,000.00 was appropriated for the Cabildo and its sister structure, the Presbytère. This latter building, seeming to be in more urgent need of major repairs, received the first attention and the bulk of the appropriation was spent in its complete rehabilitation. This work was completed under the direction of Burke, Le Breton and Lamantia, architects, and the building was reopened in 1964. The remaining portion of the funds was then spent on some essential structural repairs to the Cabildo and some replacing of deteriorated doors, windows and floors. Soon after this work was accomplished at a cost of more than $100,000.00 the city was struck by the full fury of hurricane Betsy on September 9, 1965, and much of the work that had just been completed was heavily damaged.

A delegation of interested and concerned citizens called on Governor John J. McKeithen at the Governor's mansion in Baton Rouge and were assured of his support for an appropriation of a million dollars for the Cabildo restoration. The appropriation was made in 1965 but it was reduced to $800,000 by the Capital Construction and Improvement Commission. Maxwell and Le Breton were appointed as architects with the firm of Richard Koch and Samuel Wilson, Jr. as associates. Consulting engineers were René H. Harris, Inc. with Harwood Brown doing the mechanical and electrical design and Roy Cartier the structural. Extensive research was undertaken, preliminary plans begun and in June 1966 a contract for certain demolition by way of archaeological research was awarded to Landis Construction Co. As a result of these researches and investigations, it was determined beyond doubt that most of the walls of the old French *corps de garde* had survived the fires of 1788 and 1794 and had been incorporated into the present Cabildo building. The actual floor of the French colonial structure, of bricks on edge as described by its architect Bernard Devergès, was found under

View of the Corps de Garde during the 1968-69 restoration.
Photograph by Ray Cresson.

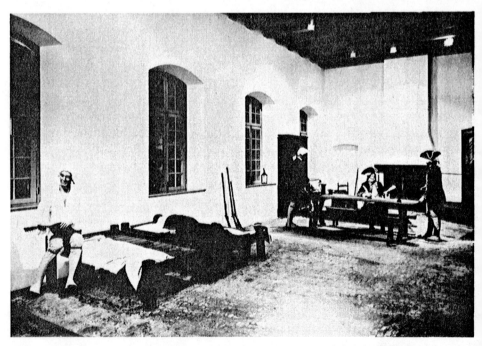

The corps de garde after restoration. The original floor of bricks laid on edge was uncovered and the fenestration restored to the appearance of the room in 1751.
Photograph by Jack Beech.

layers of later flooring. It was then decided by Mrs. Peggy Richards, the museum director, and the museum's Board of Managers that this historic oldest part of the building should be restored to its approximate appearance at the time the Cabildo was completed in 1799. This included the replacing of the small French casement windows along the St. Peter Street side and the reconstruction of the large open fireplaces on their original foundations at the end of the room. The central arcade was also restored, one of the piers that had been removed, probably when the museum was first established in 1911, being rebuilt on its old foundation.

It was decided that a plan should be developed that would provide a pattern for circulation through all the buildings of the Cabildo complex, including the Arsenal and the so-called Jackson and Creole houses. A new stair and elevator were provided to serve the various floor levels of the Cabildo and the Arsenal. The link between these two structures, built for the most part after the Arsenal, was utilized for this purpose, the Cabildo's mansard roof being extended over it to conceal the elevators and provide access to the third floor of the Cabildo.

It was also decided to restore the rooms on the second floor to their appearance at the time of the Louisiana Transfer in 1803, a restoration based on research including early plans and evidence revealed by the demolition work in the first contract. Perhaps the most interesting discovery that these investigations revealed was the location of doors opening from the front rooms to the upper gallery. Pediments, like the one surviving example, had been removed from above these doors but their size, shape and location were clearly visible in the brickwork. The third story, having been added at a much later date was to be set up for exhibition purposes, the other two stories being considered more as restored historic rooms than as exhibition spaces.

Plans and specifications were completed by the architects but, because of decreased appropriations, work on the Arsenal and the Jackson and Creole houses was listed as an alternate. Unfortunately when the bids were received, the restoration of these three buildings could not be included. The contract was awarded in June 1967, to C. B. Spencer Co., Inc. the same contractors who had done the Presbytère renovations. Their superintendent, Larry Evans, as well as Barry M. Fox and Henry W. Krotzer, Jr., of the architect's office, contributed greatly to the success of the project, which was finally completed and accepted on June 25, 1969.

The restored lamplighter's room, ground floor. The beams of the ceiling and the casement windows are original.

Photograph by Jack Beech.

In the course of the work many additional facts concerning the building were discovered. In what had at one time been the lamplighter's room on the ground floor nearest the Cathedral, an ancient floor of bricks, each about eight inches square and more than two inches thick, was discovered under the existing floor. A floor of clay tile of approximately the same size and color was then placed here. This room had retained its original beamed ceiling and its original casement windows. Its fireplace was restored on the basis of clear indications on the wall and ceiling. A new door was added on the inner wall to provide a rear access under the stair to the *corps de garde.* The two small rooms adjacent to this, originally used as the office of the notary and secretary of the Cabildo, were adapted for a staff office and public rest rooms. The main stair was left unchanged, except that the arch beneath it to the courtyard was restored and another arch added to provide a view and access to the courtyard and under the stair. Old, segmental-headed doorways found in some of the old walls in this area were reopened. In the courtyard the rear stair was enclosed in glass and louvers to provide air-conditioned access to the rear buildings and one of the former cells had to be utilized for air-conditioning equipment.

The sturdy and graceful stairway with its stone steps leads to the floors above.

Photograph by Jack Beech.

View of gallery during restoration. The marks on the wall indicate the former position of the over-door pediments.   *Photograph by Ray Cresson.*

The gallery after restoration; pediments and corbels have been restored.
Photograph by Jack Beech.

On the second floor, the gallery, with its doors and over-door pediments, was restored, as was the *Sala Capitular* and the Mayor's offices. These areas were all restored on the basis of evidence found in the fabric of the building and in careful research. The room adjacent to the *Sala Capitular*, originally divided into two smaller rooms, was left as a single space for exhibition purposes. The Mayor's parlor on the other side of the building, was restored, the design of the mantel and cornice being conjectural as was the case with these elements in the *Sala Capitular*. Two mantels installed in the Presbytère when its second story was completed in 1813 and removed in the 1961 renovations, were used in the small private office and anteroom adjacent to the Mayor's parlor. These two rooms and parts of the stair hall were the only areas on this floor that had retained their original beamed ceilings. The original beams in the other areas had apparently rotted away and been replaced and plastered over when the mansard roof was added in 1847. New beams were added to the ceiling below the structural timbers in these areas to restore the original appearance.

The mayor's parlor after restoration.

Photograph by Jack Beech.

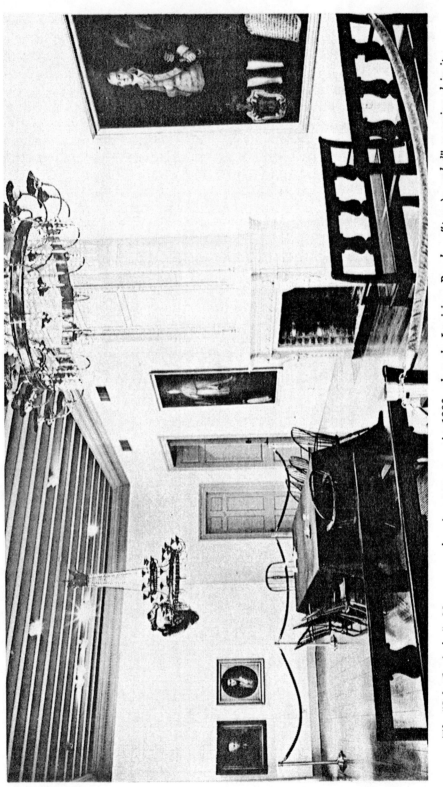

The "Sala Capitular". Now restored to its appearance in 1803 when the Louisiana Purchase "procès verbal" was signed in it.
Photograph by Jack Beech.

Anteroom of mayor's parlor.
Photograph by Jack Beech.

Corner of mayor's office.
Photograph by Jack Beech.

On the third or attic story it was found that the walls had been sheathed with huge flatboat timbers which had then been covered with split cypress laths and plastered. All the old crumbling plaster was removed and in most areas the flatboat timbers were used for the finished wall, being left exposed, together with most of the truss members, because of their unusual interest. In the upper part of the stair hall these timbers were left on the walls untouched except for cleaning and finishing, though in other areas they were reset. The great roof trusses in the large room nearest the cathedral were left exposed in so far as possible to reveal their mortise, tenon and peg construction of 1847. The old stairway leading to the cupola was left in place and extended up to a small balcony from which the trusses can be examined. The cupola, which is not open to the public, was repaired and its patterned slate roof, damaged by hurricane Betsy, was replaced as it was. The two rear attic rooms with their original 1847 mantels, were replastered in the same manner as the entire attic had been originally.

The restored third floor. The large beams and trusses were left exposed to show the method of construction.

Photograph by Jack Beech.

Detail of the third floor showing dormer window openings. The walls are covered with large planks probably from flatboats broken up when they arrived at New Orleans.

Photograph by Jack Beech.

When the entire restoration project had been completed the reopening of the Cabildo was delayed because of continuing financial difficulties. These having been at least partially solved or overcome, the date for the reopening of this National Historic Landmark was set for April 30, 1970, the anniversary of the signing of the Louisiana Purchase Treaty with France in 1803.

Bibliography

Archives Nationales, Section Outremer, Paris.

Archivo General de Indias, Seville.

Spanish Judicial Records in the Louisiana State Museum.

Miscellaneous Documents, Manuscripts Division, Library of Congress, Washington.

Reports of the Board of Police Commissioners.

Records of the Deliberations of the Cabildo (City Council) (1769-1803).

Mayors' Messages to Municipality No. 1 (1804-1853).

Journal of the Deliberations of the Council of the First Municipality.

Acts of the Louisiana Legislature.

New Orleans City Council Minutes and Resolutions.

Biennial Reports of the Board of Curators of the Louisiana State Museum (1920-1951).

Letters of Joseph Xavier Delfau de Pontalba to his wife (1796).

Stoddard, Major Amos, *Sketches, Historical and Descriptive, of Louisiana*. Philadelphia: 1812.

Ingraham, Joseph Holt, *The South-West by a Yankee*. New York: 1835.

Robin, Claude C., *Voyage to the Interior of Louisiana, 1802-1806*. Translated by Stuart O. Landry, Jr. (New Orleans, 1966).

Gibson, John, "Historical Epitome" from *Gibson's Guide and Directory of the State of Louisiana and the Cities of New Orleans and Lafayette*. New Orleans: 1838.

Latrobe, J. H. B., *Manuscript Journal in Maryland Historical Society*. Baltimore.

Latour, Major Arsène Lacarrière, *Historical Memoir of the War in West Florida and Louisiana in 1814-15*. Philadelphia: 1816.

Laussat, Pierre-Clément de, *Mémoires sur ma vie à mon fils pendant les années 1803 et suivantes* . . . Pau: 1831.

Levasseur, A. (Secretary of General Lafayette during his travels) *Lafayette in America in 1824 and 1825 or Journal of Travels in the United States*. New York: 1829.

Anonymous, *The Visit of General Lafayette in Louisiana*. New Orleans: 1825.

Wilson, Samuel, Jr., Editor, *Impressions Respecting New Orleans by Benjamin Henry Boneval Latrobe, Diary & Sketches 1818-20. New York: 1951*.

Kendall, John Smith, *History of New Orleans*. Chicago: 1922.

Fortier, Alcée, *A History of Louisiana*. New York: 1904.

Rightor, Henry, ed., *Standard History of New Orleans, Louisiana*. Chicago: 1900.

Castellanos, Henry C., *New Orleans As It Was*. New Orleans: 1895.

Fossier, Albert E., *New Orleans, the Glamour Period, 1800-1840*. New Orleans: 1957.

Carter, Hodding and Betty Werlein, *So Great a Good — a History of the Episcopal Church in Louisiana and of Christ Church Cathedral, 1805-1955*. Sewanee, Tennessee: 1955.

Newspapers

The Louisiana Courier, Louisiana Gazette, the New Orleans Daily and Weekly Delta, The Bee, The Picayune, New Orleans Times, New Orleans Republican, The Times-Democrat, The New Orleans Item, The Times-Picayune, Ballou's Pictorial Drawing Room Companion, Frank Leslie's Illustrated Newspaper.

Acknowledgments

The authors are most grateful to Miss Mary Alice Waits for her untiring efforts in researching material for this book; to René J. LeGardeur, Jr., who edited much of the text and made many useful suggestions for its improvement; to Boyd Cruise whose skillful research was of great help; to Robert G. Polack and Collin B. Hamer, Jr., head of the Louisiana Department of the New Orleans Public Library, for help in research; to the National Gallery of Art, Washington, D.C.; to Mrs. Peggy Richards, Director of the Louisiana State Museum and to Mrs. Octavie Lorio, Mrs. Aline Morris, Mrs. Sheryl Jacques, and Miss Nadine Russell of her staff for aid in research and for the loan of pictures; to Mrs. Connie G. Griffith, Head of the Special Collections and Manuscripts Department of Tulane University; to Hugh M. Wilkinson, Sr., for the loan of the miniature of General James Wilkinson; to Ray Cresson, Felix H. Kuntz and Richard Koch for use of photographs and particularly to Jack Beech who made the colored photograph of the Cabildo for the cover and the excellent pictures of the restored interior; and finally to Henry W. Krotzer, Jr., who made the authoritative restorative drawings of the first French and Spanish buildings.

The authors are deeply indebted to the Friends of the Cabildo, Incorporated, for providing the means to publish this little volume.

About the Authors

Samuel Wilson, Jr., by profession an architect and a Fellow of the American Institute of Architects, is an outstanding authority on the architectural history of Louisiana. He is a member of the faculty of Tulane University where he lectures on the history of Louisiana architecture. He is a past president and a founding member of the Louisiana Landmarks Society, and a former member of the Board of Curators of the Louisiana State Museum. He is the historian of the Orleans Parish Landmarks Commission and a member and former director of the Society of Architectural Historians.

He is the editor of *Impressions Respecting New Orleans by Benjamin Henry Boneval Latrobe* (New York, 1951), and author of *A Guide to the Architecture of New Orleans 1699-1959* (New York, 1959); "An Architectural History of the Royal Hospital and the Ursuline Convent of New Orleans," *Louisiana Historical Quarterly* (Vol. 29, No. 3, July 1946); "Louisiana Drawings by Alexandre De Batz," *Journal of the Society of Architectural Historians* (Vol. XXII, No. 3, May 1963); "Colonial Fortifications and Military Architecture in the Mississippi Valley", in *The French in the Mississippi Valley* (Urbana, Ill., 1965); "Plantation Houses on the Battlefield of New Orleans," in the *Battle of New Orleans Series* published by The Battle of New Orleans 150th Anniversary Committee of Louisiana (1965); *The Vieux Carré New Orleans, Its Plan, Its Growth, Its Architecture* (1968); *Bienville's New Orleans* (New Orleans, 1968); "Ignace François Broutin," in *Frenchmen and French Ways in the Mississippi Valley* (Urbana, Ill., 1969); and contributed essays to *New Orleans Architecture, Volume I: The Lower Garden District* (New Orleans 1971) and *New Orleans Architecture Volume II: the American Sector* (New Orleans 1972).

Leonard V. Huber is a New Orleans businessman by vocation, a historian, lecturer and collector of pictures relating to Louisiana and the Mississippi River by avocation. He is a past president of the Louisiana Landmarks Society, a member of the Society of Architectural Historians, president of the Orleans Parish Landmarks Commission and president of the Friends of the Cabildo.

He is the author or co-author of a number of books and monographs, among them *The Great Mail — a Postal History of New Orleans* (State College, Pa. 1949), *Tales of the Mississippi* (New York, 1955), "Heyday of the Floating Palace" in the October 1957 issue of *American Heritage* and "Mardi Gras—the Golden Age" in the Feb. 1965 issue of the same publication, *Advertisements of Lower Mississippi River Steamboats, 1812-1920* (New York 1960), *To Glorious Immortality — the Rise and Fall of the Girod Street Cemetery* (1961), *Citoyens, Progrès et Politique de la Nouvelle Orléans 1899-1964* (1964), "New Orleans As It Was in 1814-15" in *The Battle of New Orleans Series* published by the Battle of New Orleans 150th Anniversary Committee of Louisiana and co-editor of this series (with Charles L. Dufour — 1965), "The Golden Age of Opera, Theatre and the Performing Arts" (N. O. Magazine, Sept. 1969) and *New Orleans: A Pictorial History* (New York, 1971).

The authors have collaborated in writing *The St. Louis Cemeteries of New Orleans* (1963), *Baroness Pontalba's Buildings* (1964), *The Basilica on Jackson Square* (1965) and with Garland F. Taylor, *Louisiana Purchase* (1953).

Printed in the United States
47200LVS00005B/337-360